THE
NARROW GATE

Enjoy my tale!
Blessings,
K. L. Keith

K. L. KEITH

xulon
PRESS

Copyright © 2013 by K. L. Keith

The Narrow Gate
by K. L. Keith

Printed in the United States of America

ISBN 9781628397000

All rights reserved solely by the author. The author guarantees all contents are original and do not infringe upon the legal rights of any other person or work. No part of this book may be reproduced in any form without the permission of the author. The views expressed in this book are not necessarily those of the publisher.

Unless otherwise indicated, Bible quotations are taken from the New Living Bible Translation. Copyright © 1996 by Tyndale House Publishers.

www.xulonpress.com

DEDICATION

Praise and thanks to God, who makes all things possible to those who believe. K.L.K.

Listen to your life...
See it for the fathomless
mystery that it is.
In the boredom and pain of it no
less than in the excitement and
gladness: touch, taste, smell your
way to the holy and hidden heart
of it because in the last analysis
all moments are key moments
and life itself is grace.

Frederick Buechner

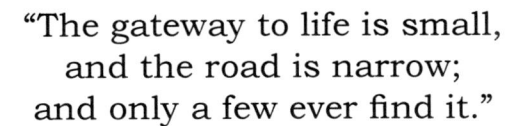

"The gateway to life is small,
and the road is narrow;
and only a few ever find it."

Matthew 7: 14

SOPHIE

(The Unimaginable)

The appointment was made last week. At that time, the thought of spending her day off sitting in the waiting room while the doctor played catch-up didn't sit well with Sophie. When she called, she asked for the earliest appointment available. "Yes, the eighth works for me, too. Nine o'clock is the first appointment of the day you said? Okay, thank you. I'll see you at nine on the eighth."

It was a beautiful May morning when she arrived at the Havendale Clinic a few minutes before nine. Billowy white clouds dotted the bright blue sky. She noticed them gliding horizontally in-step with one another, in perpetual motion, as she made her way out of the car. The morning air was still, filled with the fragrant aroma of newly blossoming Lilly of the Valley. A bird high atop a light pole warbled melodically as though performing an aria just for her. She smiled as she entered the old brick building. Oddly, Nurse Addie was nowhere in sight as she entered the reception area. She called out questioningly, "Addie?" There was no response, so she sat down to wait. She was dressed semi-casually in khaki pants and a crisply pressed white shirt. A fashionable straw hat covered her thick, shoulder length auburn hair. No other patients arrived during the brief wait-time it took for Dr. Densmore to appear and greet her like the old friend he was. "Good morning. It's nice to see you. Has it been awhile since your last visit?"

"Well, yes." She smiled. "You know I avoid coming here to see you as much as I can."

Without a response or a reaction to her attempt to be humorous, he handed her a clipboard with the standard forms to fill out. Sophie thought, *He must have a lot on his mind this morning. I'm not getting the usual playful interaction from him today.* She promptly dismissed her thoughts as she began checking the "yes" boxes for symptoms of dizziness and headaches. Just as she completed the paperwork, Dr. Densmore returned to take the information and placed a blue gown in her hand. He pointed to the changing rooms, and instructed her to report to the lab for blood work when she was ready. Sophie chuckled as she motioned to him that the changing rooms were in the opposite direction. He paused and thought for a moment before responding, "I guess it's going to be one of those days."

She left him, and soon Jessie—the portly lab technician she had known all her life—had recorded her height and weight and taken her blood pressure.

Shaking her head in disbelief, Jessie commented, "You haven't gained an ounce of weight since high school, have you?"

Sophie grinned as she jokingly replied, "I get a lot of exercise chasing down the details of all those crimes I write about, Jessie." They both grinned.

"Even if I still had them, I know I couldn't fit my big toe into the shorts we wore our senior year on the cheerleading squad," Jessie chuckled. "Come on, follow me. We're done here."

Jessie proceeded to draw blood from Sophie and then settle her on the table where she remained perfectly still for imaging scans. It was all done very efficiently, and she was pleased with the prompt attention she received.

However, within the next couple of hours, *Minneapolis Daily's* crime reporter Sophie Stangler, usually tough and stoic on the outside but soft and caring on the inside, found herself staring in disbelief at Dr. Densmore as he discussed the results of her medical tests. It seemed the frantic beating of her heart would rend her chest wide open. The tips of her fingers tingled and began to grow numb. Nausea threatened to overtake her. A trickle of warm sweat streamed down her back. She struggled to listen to his words. She was fighting to remain standing upright. As Dr. Densmore continued to speak, his words became muffled and slightly muted, taking on a faraway, dream-like quality. It was as though he were speaking balderdash. She could no longer make out what he was saying. Her thoughts were a million miles away. Bewildered and on the verge of panic, she tried to process her thoughts on how to handle all this. Her job demanded that she act decisively and always move forward in a take-charge manner. This had nothing to do with her job. She felt like a fish out of water. Her mind was flooded with so many questions: *What do I do first? How will I do justice to each day I have left? Who do I tell? Who do I try to shield and protect from the agony of knowing? Mom and Dad, I can' tell them. It would be too painful for them.*

Parents aren't supposed to outlive their children, even their adult children. It can't be a malignant brain tumor! Is this really happening to me? Heavenly Father, I ask you to please give me the answers and the strength I need to get through this. At that moment, the fear and disbelief were overwhelming, and she lost consciousness.

Outside the Havendale Clinic, spring was unfolding in the bright warm morning sun. People were going about their lives blissfully unaware of the drama unfolding in Sophie's life. The southern Wisconsin air was thick with the sweet scent of lilacs. Lush flower-covered boughs of snowy white spirea fanned out and bent down as if bowing to the locals passing by on their way to work. Tourists seeking the nostalgia of a bygone era began arriving by bus. Anticipating a fun day out, small groups of women parked their cars along the banks of the placid St. Thomas River. In search of their first good, strong cup of coffee of the day, they began milling about the red cobblestone streets of the historic downtown area. Like a magnet, the scent of freshly ground coffee beans drew them to bustling coffee shops. Proprietors of cozy antique stores and the quaint shops lining Main Street paused while sweeping their front stoops to turn and acknowledge their visitors. "Good morning. Isn't this a beautiful morning?" Merchants turned their window signs to "open", and donned their aprons in anticipation of another business day.

The spring rains arrived earlier than usual this year and washed away winter's mantle of dust and debris. Left behind were lush, green, rolling hillsides. Multicolored Victorian mansions, clad in clapboard siding adorned with fish-scale shingles and lace-trimmed roofs, cheerily lined the narrow neighborhood streets. After a long winter nap at the Habersham Boat Yard just north of town, skiffs and sailboats sat moored in the clear water. The tepid breeze caused them to rock gently back and forth. It was peaceful and calm throughout the charming little river town which Sophie called home.

When Sophie regained consciousness, Dr. Densmore was standing beside her bedside. Reluctantly, she lifted her eyes and looked directly into his mournful face. She had known him most of her life. He had taken care of her family since they moved to Havendale when she was just five years old...forty-five years ago. He and her father became good friends over the years. She saw him as a treasured part of their family. As she continued to look into his eyes, she somehow managed to see beyond herself and sensed the pain and utter helplessness that had overtaken him. In that moment, she grieved for this kind compassionate man whom she knew wanted desperately to offer her hope and healing. She wanted to reach out to him in some way, but she was unable to offer him any comfort. Barely able to find her voice, Sophie asked, "How much time do I have?"

SADIE

(Earlier That Morning)

*P*retty, petite Sadie Harrington hit the ground running most mornings. As a wife and mother of three, she packed more in one day than most people accomplished in two! Before she married Ted, her high school sweetheart, she was a nurse at the hospital in Havendale. For the past twenty-odd years, she had been a stay-at-home mom while her two boys and daughter were growing up. Unlike some of her peers who gave up their careers to stay at home when their children were born, she never felt it was a sacrifice. That was where she wanted to be.

It was five o'clock in the morning, and unlike her usual pattern of bounding out of bed after a peaceful night's sleep, she hadn't been able to sleep. She had quietly left Ted sleeping peacefully, and gone down to the sun porch to sit in the early morning sun. Feeling the warmth of the sun as it kissed her face, her thoughts rambled.

She recalled herself saying to Ted before they were married so many years ago, *I don't think there is any job as important as raising healthy children. Our kids will need me, and I plan to stay home and be a full-time parent.* They were both grateful that Ted, a mechanical engineer, was able to provide the financial support needed for the five of them to live a comfortable life on the north hill, the oldest and most historic area of Havendale.

She then started to think about how much she loved this sun room. They bought the house shortly after they were married, and Ted wanted to knock out the adjoining living room wall to make the sun porch and the living room into one large den. She had stood firm, and convinced him they needed to leave everything intact. In her mind, she could hear herself saying to him: *No, sweetheart, this sun porch is actually going to become my favorite room in the whole house. I know I will be spending as much time as I can right here in this lovely room with our babies.* From the beginning, she felt the house was perfect for them just as it was. In those early years of their marriage, the sun porch did become a special place where she cooed and sang to her babies. She smiled as she recalled images from so long ago when she cradled them in her arms and lulled them to sleep. The memory of gently rocking back and forth in the ornate wicker rocking chair that sat directly across from her in the corner of the room was so vivid, she could almost feel it. The double-caned rocker, so lovingly restored, was handed down from her grandparents to her parents. They passed it on to her with the birth of her oldest child, Seth. Her face lit up at the sight of it, and for a brief moment, her mind once again was flooded with precious memories of their early days in this house as young parents.

When the kids were little, she was selflessly dedicated to taking an active, guiding role in all their activities. She had been the kind of mom who baked something special for each of them to take to school as a special treat on their birthdays. She was there when they returned home from school each day, and she had a special way of making them feel treasured and loved. Nothing was more important to her than her family. That was the way it had been for her when she was a young girl growing up in Havendale with her sister, Sophie. That was the gift she wanted to give her children as well. Her life back then was good, and she always felt if she could be just half the parent her parents had been, she would have succeeded as a parent.

A giggle escaped her lips and tickled her with glee as she traveled back in thought once again to the day of Seth's sixth birthday. *It was a school day. At his request, I baked and decorated a dinosaur cake to take to school as a special treat for his classmates. The cake was on a rectangular cardboard platter. I put considerable thought into how I would get the cake to school without any mishaps. I remember carefully and very strategically placing it on the back seat of the car, wedging it between things, to hold it in place. As we drove to J. G. Henning Elementary School, Seth was highly animated and chatted excitedly about the coming day. I, on the other hand, felt somewhat melancholy about my little boy growing up so fast. I drove more slowly than usual, and the trip was going well until we reached the approach to the school. Suddenly, and seemingly out of nowhere, a little boy darted in front of the car. I can still see the look of innocent eagerness on his face! It was his turn to share at show-and-tell, and he was on a mission to get to his classroom as fast as he could. In his arms, he clutched Elmer, his new black and white stuffed puppy. Oh, thank God,*

I was able to slam on the brake and stop the car in time.

Then she laughed aloud as she continued recalling the incident. *My beautiful cake took flight. I can still see it hurling through the air, landing on my lap, covering me and the front seat with multicolored frosting!* Shaking her head, she thought, *Thank goodness, those days are behind me.*

At forty-eight, Sadie was the younger of the two sisters. Her indomitable spirit and outgoing personality often overshadowed Sophie. Everyone loved her. Ted was more in love with her today than the day he married her. They had grown comfortable with each other over the years, but not complacent in their relationship. The magic was still there. They had just recently celebrated their 25th anniversary by renewing their wedding vows. Conjuring up the memory of the tender words he had spoken to her now brought tears of overwhelming humility to her eyes. *"You are the best thing that's ever happened to me. Without you, I would be nothing. I love you more now than I ever have, and I will love you forever."*

Oh, how I love that good man. It just gets better and better with him. Thank you, Lord. Thank you for the blessing of my wonderful man. It was a lavish two-day celebration at their home that included the kids, many of their closest friends, and family members.

I'm so grateful to be blessed in so many ways. I'm especially grateful for the way the kids are pursuing their interests and ambitions, preparing themselves to become contributing adults in society. A pleasant smiled adorned her face as a soft sigh escaped.

Her thoughts rambled on. *When Christian, my baby, left for college in the fall, I did briefly give some thought to going back to work. Silly me! My nursing skills are such a faint memory. It's extremely unlikely there would have been a place for me in the job market. Thankfully, I threw myself into volunteering at the hospital reading to children in the pediatric ward instead. How quickly I became attached to all of them. I adore seeing their faces light up as we share the make believe adventures of their favorite story book characters. It makes me feel so good to be a small part of their lives. I treasure being able to bring them some comfort and a brief escape from their pain and illness as we travel to far-off places in the pages of the books we share.*

She grew to know their families, too, and often spent time with them at the hospital listening, or speaking soft, loving words of hope and encouragement in their most desperate hours. *I so often find myself reaching deep in my inner core, trying hard to put myself in their place in an attempt to find the empathy and sensitivity they need from me at those times. I am so touched when they speak to me of God and His loving presence in their lives in their most vulnerable times. So many times I've seen how the knowledge of that presence brings them renewed strength and courage. They are so special to me. Spending time at the hospital with these incredible people brings abundant joy and so much purpose and fulfillment to my life.*

Sitting alone now with just her thoughts, wrapped in the pillow-like softness of the down-filled sofa cushions, Sadie repeatedly thought to herself, *I feel so grateful for the joy it brings me to be a part of these wonderful people's lives.*

Too quickly though, she was drawn back to the nagging thoughts that had caused her to toss and turn in sleeplessness and rise so early. Something didn't feel right, and the feeling had caused her to rise and linger here in solitude. She couldn't begin to identify what it was or make sense of the feeling that had come over her. *What is it? Why am I so restless? Why do I have this nagging feeling that something sinister is lurking in ominous shadows and surrounding me?*

Closing her striking blue eyes—which were now red from lack of sleep—she prayed aloud, "Please, Lord, keep my family safe from harm. I don't know if these thoughts and feelings I'm having are real, but if they are a forewarning of something evil to come, I ask you to fight for my loved ones. Protect them from all evil. I ask this in the loving and powerful name of Jesus. Amen."

It would be months later—not later that day during her upcoming lunch date with Sophie—when a searing beam of reality would burn through her; exposing the heart-wrenching truth threatening her loved one.

MARCUS
(Blissfully Happy)

At the time Sophie was meeting with Dr. Densmore across town, young Marcus Crandall, an up-and-coming CPA at the firm of Hyshum and Lester, was just pulling into the parking lot at work. The firm was located in the old courthouse that sat high atop the south hill. The courthouse was built in the 1800s, and was listed on the National Historic Register. A massive renovation project had turned it into a modern day high-rise. It now featured intricately patterned parquet floors; elaborate crown moldings; paneled cherry woodwork; beveled mirrors; polished marble; brass hardware; and exquisite antique

The Narrow Gate

light fixtures. The restoration of the exterior, too, had been masterfully done. The old tastefully melded with the new. This was required for historic buildings by the state of Wisconsin. It was one among the many acclaimed architectural jewels in Havendale. Hyshum and Lester occupied the fifth floor, enjoying a breathtaking view overlooking Havendale and the peaceful water of the beautiful St. Thomas River.

Marcus joined the firm shortly after passing the rigorous tests that promoted him to CPA status two years ago. Young and eager to prove himself, he was still as enthused about going to work as he had been back then. Initially, he had been assigned to work with some of the firm's mid-size corporate accounts. However, a couple of months ago one of the senior partners, Dick Lester, had reassigned him to work exclusively on the Hovland account. It was one of their major corporate accounts. His diligence, hard work, and unusually keen sense of business had paid off and landed him the promotion.

He smiled as he recalled Dick's words, *"You earned it, Marcus. You've become a strong asset to the company. Keep up the good work."*

He clicked the remote to lock his car and continued thinking as he walked toward the lobby. *The relocation to Wisconsin really turned out to be a good move for Molly and me. I'm sure glad about that since she was so reluctant to leave our hometown and her family back in Maine. I wasn't crazy about leaving my family behind either. My parents have grown to depend on me more as they've grown older, but the poor economy in Maine made it necessary for us to make the move.*

They were both thirty-three years old. Their nine-year marriage was a match made in heaven. Now, after trying to have a baby for the past seven years, they found themselves anticipating becoming parents. Molly would have a C-section in just two weeks: May 22. They were ecstatic!

The Narrow Gate

Both of them were beside themselves with excitement and gratitude.

The main floor of the courthouse was available to rent for weddings, receptions, and other events. Their neighbors had recently thrown a large, surprise, couples baby shower for them there that included coworkers from his firm. In the excitement of it all, Marcus' playful side had surfaced, replacing his usually reserved demeanor. As he traveled back in his mind to that day, he recalled having a wonderful time in spite of the silly games they made him play. He reran the scene in his mind. *Blindfolded, spun around in circles, and set forth to pin the diaper on the doll, I wasn't even able to find the large, life-like doll let alone pin a diaper on it!* Echoes of their hysterical laughter playing in his mind made him chuckle aloud.

At home, the large walk-in closet just off their bedroom was recently renovated and turned into the nursery. It was freshly painted in a soothing combination of cream and soft mint green with coordinating striped wallpaper hung on one wall. Thanks to their families in Maine, it was filled with all the necessary essentials for the baby's first six months. Plush receiving blankets, miniature bodysuits, and snuggly-soft sleepers were laid out in anticipation of the trip home from the hospital. Adorable Winnie the Pooh comforters, curtains, and rugs adorned the room.

They hadn't wanted to know ahead of time if they were having a boy or a girl, so they were ready with the name Claire Christine for a daughter and Christopher Robin for a son. They were taking a little ribbing from his grandparents on the Christopher Robin name, but it didn't bother either of them. His grandfather called weekly and teased, "You know, if you name that baby Christopher Robin you're going to have to get him a bear, a piglet, and an owl to play with."

Like many first-time fathers, Marcus was secretly hoping for a boy, and he often found himself wondering if Molly, too, was wishing for a girl. If she was, she had been uncharacteristically successful in keeping the secret to herself. Their daily conversations centered on the baby, but she hadn't said a word about it.

It was one of the happiest times of their lives. Marcus had to consciously shake off the always present, blissful thoughts of becoming a father.

Climbing the steps and reaching for the front door, he entered the lobby with a smile on his face and a heart brimming with love. He had no idea the euphoric feeling coursing through him would be a fleeting high, soon turning to darkness that would come crashing down around him.

DR. JACK DENSMORE
(Unable To Offer Hope)

"It's hard to say, Sophie, perhaps six months." Dr. Densmore responded. "But people have beaten the odds. I could send you to see a brain specialist at Mayo Clinic."

His voice sounds flat and unlike him, thought Sophie. "Jack, I need you to be totally honest with me. Do you truly feel there is even a slight chance something could be done?"

The strained look on his face spoke volumes to her, and she knew the answer to her question before he managed to utter his reply. "No," he said with complete devastation as he shook his head. "The scans show a deeply lodged tumor. It's inoperable."

The Narrow Gate

His words cut through Sophie, leaving her momentarily speechless, as she lowered her head and closed her eyes. The recent headaches and dizziness made sense to her now. Slowly, she looked up at him, took a deep breath, and nodded her head as she whispered, "Ok...ok."

There it was, the cold, harsh truth fully exposed. Throughout her life, she had always said she would rather be hurt with the truth than with a lie. Being honest had always been important to Sophie. She had a remarkable reputation among her coworkers for being doggedly determined in searching out the absolute truth in every story she reported.

Reaching out to help her sit up, Dr. Densmore caringly said, "Let's move into my office where we can talk."

For the next hour, the truth hit her hard as they talked at great length about what she could expect in the coming months. In the end, he started to write out a prescription, but stopped to study it for a while. Sophie watched as he tore the sheet from the pad. He threw it away and began writing again.

He handed this one to her saying, "This medication should help control the dizziness and reduce the headaches for a while."

Numbly, Sophie reached out to take it from him.

"I'm sorry, Sophie." Then he flatly uttered the words, "Nurse Addie isn't here right now. Would you like me to call someone to drive you home—Sadie, perhaps?"

For the first time since her arrival, Sophie noticed the time. The noon hour was approaching, and as she stood to leave, her thoughts returned to the outside world. "No, I'll be all right. I'm meeting her for lunch, and the drive will give me some time to compose myself. I don't want her to know just yet, Jack. She doesn't know I'm here," Sophie continued.

He nodded his understanding, and she turned and left his office. As she walked in a dazed state to her car, the brilliant, blue sky above and the sweet aroma of the fresh, pink, blossoming

Crabapple trees lining the parking lot went unnoticed.

SOPHIE

(Reflections)

*O*nce inside her car, Sophie closed her eyes and began to breathe deeply. After five deep breaths, she opened her eyes. Turning her head and looking out the front passenger window, she noted nothing within view had changed since her arrival at the clinic. "Yet," she said aloud, "my life has been irreversibly altered. I am dying, and I now have the answers to the mystery of both how and approximately when I will die. Wow! Wow!" For a fleeting moment, thoughts of a lifesaving scenario began to fill her mind. Nevertheless, the trust she held in Dr. Densmore's reputation and medical experience led her to accept that it was real and final. *He's one of the best. He's known throughout the state for his innate ability to predict his patient's conditions to a high degree of accuracy even before receiving the confirming results of their medical tests. No, there is no going back for further tests and second opinions. I need to accept it for what it is.* One more deep breath followed, and she inserted the key in the ignition, backed her car out of the parking lot, and headed for Miss Dazie's Restaurant.

Round and round in her mind, her thoughts tumbled, like clothes whirling and spinning out of control in the dryer. *How will I face Sadie at lunch without revealing the anguished thoughts and emotions that are saturating me? Can I even do it? Maybe I should call her and cancel. What would I say? What reason would I give her? Wait a minute, she's my sister. Shouldn't I want to turn to her for comfort and support? Shouldn't she be the one person I would want to help me carry this burden?* Of the two of them, she had always been emotionally *stronger. Not yet. I think perhaps it might be best to shelter Sadie from the truth as long as I can. Besides, even if I could find the words to tell her, I'm not sure I could say them out loud.*

She moved her foot off the accelerator to slow down as she approached Poppy Street, where the light had turned red, and her car crawled to a stop.

I wonder if the feelings I'm having are normal. Is there a normal way to feel and react to the news that I have just months to live? No, I'm right to hold off saying anything for now. It's premature to share the news with Sadie. I haven't had a chance to process any of it yet, myself; and I certainly don't want to tell her something like this in a public place.

Consumed in thought, she didn't notice that the light had turned green until an impatient driver behind her sounded his horn. It startled her, and made her realize the need to pay closer attention to her driving.

As she drove on and approached Seventh Avenue, she passed the old bank building so elegantly bathed in magnificent neoclassic architecture. Replaced by the need for a larger and more modern facility, the stately old building now housed a unique collection of quaint shops that attracted both locals and tourists. Further up, at the corner of Mill and State Street, was the old Bloomfield Mill. Made of limestone, it had once been a bustling flour mill; but today it hosted a popular tea room. Turning onto Main Street, the festive red-and-white striped awning of Wilma's Bakery caught her eye. The rusty, red brick building had been a cornerstone on Main Street for as long as she could remember. She heard the ringing of a bell, and for a brief moment, her attention was drawn to the trolley car parked in front of the bakery. She watched as an assortment of tourists debarked and lined up at the front door. For reasons unknown to Sophie, it brought her comfort to gaze at these old familiar landmarks. She loved everything about them...their charming, old-fashioned Victorian features, their history, and the lively

Sophie

tales she knew so well of their place in a long-ago bygone era. The quaint cobblestone walks and the old street lamps lining them warmed her heart, almost bringing a faint smile to her troubled face. Havendale truly was a special place to her, and she loved it dearly.

As she approached the south end of Main Street, Miss Dazie's Restaurant came into view. Perched along the banks of the river, the rustic old railroad depot had survived disabling spring floods and the abandonment of a once thriving rail line. Its most recent reincarnation as a restaurant was a robust success! The restaurant featured both inside and outside dining on the deck, and gave eager patrons the experience of enjoying the taste of the best homemade comfort food found for miles around. They could also enjoy the flavor of life on the river in the 1800s. Whimsically-painted replicas of 20th century steamboats plied the St. Thomas. On board were locals, tourists, church groups, wedding parties, and business and civic groups. Each vessel provided its patrons breathtaking views of the natural, undisturbed, rolling hillsides now budding with new life. The seven ornate church steeples peeking out amongst the trees on both the north and south hill completed the picture.

Steering her car into the parking lot, Sophie noticed Sadie's car. She gasped as a twinge of fear momentarily overtook her. "Breathe, Sophie Beth, breathe," she recited under her breath. "You can do this. You can. God has not made you with a spirit of fear but of strength and soundness of mind." Over the years, she had often pumped herself up by reciting her paraphrased version of this Bible verse. It had become one of her favorites. It sustained her and helped her overcome tough challenges when ferreting out the elusive truth as a crime reporter for the *Minneapolis Daily*. She knew firsthand the powerful effect of a positive, can-do attitude, and she drew upon that belief now as she unlatched her seatbelt and boldly headed out the door.

QUINN
(Lifelong Friend)

As she entered the restaurant, Sophie heard Quinn Dazie's amiable voice before actually laying eyes on her. Suddenly, Quinn appeared from around the corner. She greeted her childhood friend with a warm hello and an adoring smile as she threw her arms around Sophie, wrapping her in a loving embrace. "Hello, my dear friend. I'm so glad to see you." At five-foot-nine, she was strikingly beautiful. Masterfully-applied makeup and an exquisite fashion sense enhanced her already naturally beautiful features. The combination of her large deep-set brown eyes and honey blond hair, pulled straight back in a soft flowing ponytail, gave her an air of simple elegance. Sophie cherished the moment and returned the embrace with genuine affection.

For a brief moment, her mind was filled with the vision of their first meeting when a five-year-old Quinn, standing at the edge of her driveway, nervously asked Sophie to be her friend. She had never forgotten the uneasy look on Quinn's anguished young face as she had made her gallant request: *"Do you think you and me might could be friends and play together when I come out of the house?"* Their families had moved to Havendale around the same time, although Sophie's family had arrived about a month before the Dazie family. In her unfamiliar surroundings, Quinn had seemed desperate for a friend. Sophie remembered responding to her request resolutely, *"Yes, and I think we could still be friends inside the house, too."* Her innocent response laid claim to what became a predestined, through thick-and-thin, lifelong relationship.

The two little neighbor girls became fast friends, making the most of their carefree summer days riding their bicycles, roller skating, playing hopscotch and doing all of the other activities of their time.

Throughout elementary school and high school they were inseparable, but after graduation, they went in different directions. A confident, determined Sophie attended the nearby University of Minnesota, majoring in both criminology and journalism. Quinn traveled extensively and lived in Europe. The friendship forged early in their young lives left treasured memories that always kept them close despite the geographic distance between them.

Quinn's life had been full of adventure. Through it all, she remained the same down-to-earth, genuine friend Sophie had learned to cherish so many years ago. They faithfully exchanged birthday and Christmas cards. Quinn's impeccable timing with her monthly phone calls had often been just the pick-me-up

The Narrow Gate

Sophie needed. When Quinn traveled back to Havendale for a visit, she always stayed with Sophie, and they spent most of their time reminiscing and basking in the gift of just being together.

Quinn returned to Havendale a year ago. Opening her own restaurant was a dream-come-true for her. It was wonderful having her back home, and it felt wonderful holding her close. Pulling away from the embrace, Sophie, too, responded with a warm, "Hello, my precious friend."

Quinn quickly took Sophie's hand as she motioned for Sophie to follow her. Heading around the corner, she informed Sophie she had already seated Sadie in the main dining room at a table overlooking the river. Casting an amused backward glance at Sophie, she impishly stated, "She has a surprise for you. You'll love it!"

A sudden sense of discomfort came over Sophie as she began searching the room for their table. A pure and intense sense of relief washed over her as she caught sight of Sadie and her daughter, Sydney, smiling and waving to them. "Thank you, Lord," she whispered under her breath. She knew their attention at lunch would center on Sydney, not her. The welcome distraction would enable her to get through lunch without alerting Sadie to the new development in her life.

MARCUS

(Embezzlement)

Back at the CPA firm of Hyshum and Lester, the morning had passed quickly for Marcus. Pushing himself away from his desk, he rose and cast a glance at his watch. It was time to break for lunch, but he was distracted by a nagging sense of doubt and apprehension. Some of the data on the latest reports on the Hovland account had become intensely disturbing. It had dulled his appetite and dampened the euphoric mood he experienced earlier.

When Dick Lester assigned him to the account, he had reassigned Danny Lockwood. Danny had clearly been resentful over his reassignment and hadn't gotten over it. Marcus had repeatedly e-mailed Danny with questions about the account. He stewed as he mentally recreated Danny's characteristic written responses, *I can't remember. Figure it out for yourself.*

When he saw Danny in the hall or around the building, there was always a reason why he just didn't have time to talk to Marcus. Marcus tried to be patient and accepting. *I really thought I could eventually soothe Danny's feelings and make peace between us. It didn't take me long to realize that wasn't going to happen. There was just no winning Danny over.* So Marcus continued on alone, working hard to familiarize himself with all aspects of the diversity of the account. He learned all the intricate plans for growth and expansion without the benefit of Danny's input. About a month into taking over the account, Marcus began to have a sense there might be impending trouble with some of the figures. He would need to delve further in order to bring the problem to light. He found himself thinking,

Today's reports confirm things are more serious than I originally suspected. He was now becoming deeply troubled.

Feeling the need for fresh air, he headed toward the door. As he entered the hallway, Simon Hanson, known to everyone as Si, was coming out of his office just across from him. They gently bumped shoulders. Marcus didn't want to let on to Si that he was worried about what Danny was possibly doing with the account, so he jokingly said, "Hey, nice running into you, man."

With a serious look on his face, Simon asked, "What are you working on?"

"Nothing too important right now; just found a little kink in one of my accounts. I'm taking a break and heading out to the balcony to get some fresh air. Come on out and join me for a few minutes."

"No, I can't. I'm on my way out. I have to meet a client for lunch," Simon replied.

Relieved that he would not be forced to make small talk with him, Marcus turned to walk away as he casually promised to set up a golf date with him soon. When Molly and he moved to Havendale, Si had been a big help to them. It was on Si's recommendation that they hired the real estate agent who found their new house. He also introduced him around town to some of the more prominent business owners. However, in spite of their early history, Si remained distant—they had never become close friends. Marcus always found him somewhat hard to talk to.

Marcus exited the building and stood alongside the wrought iron railing on the small, isolated balcony outside. He often came here to drink in the fresh air and clear his head, while taking in the breathtaking view of the St. Thomas and the thick pine trees covering the deep ravine below.

Troubling thoughts soon filled his head again. *I have enough evidence to confront Danny. Unbelievable! What was Danny thinking? I don't doubt Danny cooked those books! Embezzlement! What possible motive*

The Narrow Gate

could he have had? What made him think he could possibly get away with it?

He struggled with thoughts of the possibility that there was some logical explanation, but deep in his heart, he knew that couldn't be true. *What possible legitimate reason could there be for a half-million dollar deficit in funds? Danny is too good an accountant to make that kind of mistake. No, he was clever in covering up the discrepancies.*

Still conflicted, Marcus apprehensively knew what he had to do. *I have to tell Dick. He needs to know, and I need his help in confronting Danny. Well, maybe before I do that, I should speak to Danny confidentially. Maybe, just maybe he can put a different spin on this. This is unbelievable!*

He was just about to turn and reenter the building to see if Danny was in his office when, out of nowhere, a crushing blow drove him forward. In an instant, he lost his balance and hit the wrought iron railing in front of him with such force that he catapulted into the air. Without a sound, he fell to the steep ravine below. Marcus Crandall's life and troubled heart were gone.

SYDNEY

(A Bride-To-Be)

Sydney arose from her chair at Miss Dazies and eagerly reached out to embrace the woman who had been like a second mother to her. She adored her Aunt Sophie, and was genuinely glad to see her. "What a fabulous surprise to see you, sweetheart," Sophie said. "Your mother didn't tell me you were coming home."

"It was a surprise to me, too," added Sadie, as she also stood to welcome her big sister with a warm embrace. "I'm as pleasantly surprised as you are."

Sophie looked back at Sydney and noticed she was positively aglow and grinning from ear to ear. The special closeness they had shared since Sydney was a little girl was due in part to Sophie's uncanny ability to read her like a book. However, it wouldn't have taken the instincts of a professional crime solver to know she was here to share news of something wonderful going on in her life.

As the three of them sat down and began to settle in, Sophie crossed her arms in front of her chest, leaned back in her chair, and raised her eyebrows. She gave Sydney an exaggerated nod and a look that silently spoke the message: *You're not leaving here until I get every last exciting detail, young lady.*

Sydney responded with a giggle as if she had been waiting on stage for her cue. "I'm engaged!" she gushed.

Sophie was absolutely astounded. "You're engaged? But I thought Michael had convinced you to wait until you both graduated," she replied with genuine disbelief.

"I know, I know," Sydney beamed. "But he got this fabulous offer from the head of the Sleep Disorders Department at Stanford, and he just couldn't pass it up. He said he wasn't moving to California without me, so we're getting married December 8. Oh, Aunt Sophie, I want you to be my maid of honor!" she squealed.

Sophie froze. Panic threatened to overcome her as she struggled to stifle the devastating thoughts of her impending mortality. In all likelihood, she wouldn't even be here next December. Looking into Sydney's beautiful innocent face, the reality of her situation hit hard. She struggled to find the words to respond. It took all her will to catch her breath and quell the myriad of feelings running rampant inside her. "What about all of your friends from college? Wouldn't you really rather have one of them as your maid of honor?"

Sydney didn't miss a beat in her reply, and it became apparent to Sophie she had given it a great deal of thought. "There is no one who has been as special to me as you, Aunt Sophie. I have loved you and admired you my whole life, and there is no one I would rather have standing by my side on the most important day of my life. You've been such a significant part of my life. I would be so honored if you would accept."

"Oh, Sydney." Overwhelmed by Sydney's outpouring of love, Sophie leaned forward. The two of them embraced as Sophie heard herself whisper, "Of course I'll be your maid of honor." Sophie closed her eyes, hoping to stop the flood of tears she felt coming on.

It was Sadie who, unknowingly, broke in and saved her from the onslaught of tears threatening to expose the raw emotion about to pour out of her. "That's enough you two! Let's order lunch. I'm starving."

Just then, Quinn arrived at their table with four tall glasses of strawberry lemonade and announced, "This is my lucky day. I get to dine with you lovely ladies."

The three of them delighted in their time together, reminiscing and recounting for Sydney the secrets of their innocent, youthful antics.

The Narrow Gate

"Do you remember the time we took white paint from your dad's garage and painted an extra zero on the population sign on the south entrance of town?" Quinn comically reminisced with a wink and a devilish look. Both Sophie and Sadie quickly tried to shush her, but soon the three of them burst into laughter as they looked at Sydney.

Sydney's face was agog in wonderment over the revealing news of their youthful shenanigans and eagerly encouraged Quinn: "Don't you dare hold anything back. I want all the mischievous, juicy details!"

"Okay, my pleasure! There was the time we switched the sign for the Rollie Hotel with the local nursing home!" Quinn stated, wide-eyed. She could hardly continue telling the rest of the story. "We hid in the park for a while to see what would happen. In the time we were there, four different parties showed up with their suitcases wanting to rent a room for the night! As we huddled together thinking about the conversation they were having inside with the nursing home staff, we laughed so hard we fell over in a heap on the ground!"

The four of them could barely contain themselves, and over the next several hours, the laughter and chatter coming from their table never stopped. It turned out to be a marvelous afternoon for all of them. When it was over, Sophie especially felt refreshed and energized by the warmth of the bond between them. She was also weak from laughter. The afternoon was a blessing she had not anticipated. It brought her just what she needed. She felt oddly peaceful and a little more ready to start facing the demon growing inside her.

RALPH AND STELLA

(A Step Back In Time)

Driving through Main Street while heading towards home, Sophie entertained the idea of packing a bag and heading to her cottage for the weekend. She had taken the day off to meet with Dr. Densmore, so she hadn't planned to go back to the office. It was an absolutely gorgeous afternoon. The buds on the trees were noticeably unwrapping, displaying abundant new life. Above, the clouds had moved out, and the sky was perfectly clear. The temperature had warmed up to a pleasant 72 degrees. The Thursday night weather forecast called for unseasonably high temperatures for the next four to five days. With her parents out of town—celebrating the fiftieth wedding anniversary of her mother's old college roommate—she had no other plans for the weekend. Everything seemed to fall into place, so at the traffic light just ahead, she turned into Ralph's Standard Station to gas up the car for the two hour drive.

For just a brief moment, she thought, *The day will come when I will no longer be able to drive.* Quickly, she shook off the dismal thought and began waving to Ralph who was sitting on an old, three-legged wooden stool. She carefully steered her car up to the outside pump. There were only two pumps located opposite each other, standing like sentries, under a red tile roof which extended out from the whitewashed stucco building like a portico. One was red and one was green. Just opposite the pumps, an ornate screen door, no doubt dressed in its original coat of green paint, added to the nostalgia of the unique station. Ralph and Stella Mosley had owned and operated Ralph's since 1959. It was virtually a step back in

The Narrow Gate

time. Little had changed since they opened the business. It proudly stood to represent one of the last bastions where patrons still received personal service from the owners. They were both well into their eighties in age, yet they greeted every customer with a cheery smile and an eagerness to serve them. Of course they knew many of their customers because they were locals who, like Sophie and her family, stopped in regularly and ran a tab. The station also saw many tourists and out-of-towners stopping in on a daily basis in the warm weather months. It didn't matter to Ralph and Stella. They treated everyone the same, making a personal connection to each customer and chatting away as if they had known them a long time, while courteously pumping their gas and cleaning their windows.

Sophie lowered her window and turned to greet Ralph. "Hey there, young fellow," she called out. "Fill 'er up with regular, would you, please?"

Ralph adjusted his cap and willingly got up off his stool. He lowered his head, positioning himself to get a good look at the driver as he walked closer to Sophie's car. He soon recognized her and responded with a playful, "Anything for you good lookin'. I'm always glad to see my favorite crime-solving reporter."

Ralph and Stella had followed Sophie's career since she started writing for the *Minneapolis Daily*, and they were among her biggest fans. They had worked day and night at the station for most of their lives. A few years back, after the three of them had talked until they were blue in the face, they finally convinced Eugene, their stubborn, reluctant nephew, to fill in for them at the station for a day. Sophie picked them up around 8:00 a.m. the next morning, and drove them to the *Daily*. She and various coworkers conducted a full tour of the landmark. Ralph and Stella had both been thrilled to meet and talk with her well-known editor and boss, Colin Edwards. They had gotten autographs from daily columnists Eva Patterson and Fred Wilson. She thought about how famed sports writer, Sig Roswell, *got the biggest kick out of the chastisement Ralph gave him about his recent column on the Minnesota Twins. "Remember, ya gotta always make the home team look good." Ralph said in sincere seriousness. "I know they didn't play good that last game with our Wisconsin boys, but they're your boys. Them's the only ones you got. Make 'em always look good, and you'll do fine."* Sophie laughed right out loud as she reminisced about that now. *I don't recall that either of them has had a day off since that outing,* she mused. Ralph started the pump, and Sophie raised her window as he came around to wash it.

When he was finished, she lowered it again and inquired about Stella. "She's doing real good. I expect she's tending to Mr. Dievers just now. He isn't too patient when he wants something, and Stella is too kind-hearted to deny him," he said with a nod and a charming twinkle in his eye. Mr. Dievers was Stella's cat and longtime companion. The couple had no children, so the three of them were a family, and Stella shamelessly pampered both of them to no end.

When he finished, Ralph slowly replaced the nozzle and twisted the cap on her gas tank as Sophie called out, "Give her my best, and remind her I'll be by next week to settle up my tab."

Ralph turned to smile at her and said, "I'll tell her. You drive careful now, ya' hear?"

A receipt wasn't necessary. Running a tab had always worked out just fine. Before the end of each month, she stopped by to pay up and have coffee with Stella. She always enjoyed that time with Stella. As Sophie drove off, she was struck with thoughts of just how much she was looking forward to visiting with her sometime within the next few weeks.

They live such a simple life. They work hard, but they always seem to be content and happy. I love the way their happiness rubs off on me when I'm with them. I guess that's why I always leave feeling uplifted after being with them.

SOPHIE

(The Cabin)

*H*eading west up the hill from Main Street towards home, Sophie's thoughts turned toward affirming that it really was a good idea for her to head to the cottage. *If the outcome of my appointment with Dr. Densmore had turned out differently, I would have thought of it earlier.* She was always anxious to begin another summer season at the lake so she had already opened the cabin a couple of weeks ago in anticipation.

She bought what she called her "little slice of heaven" after realizing it wasn't realistic for her to think she was ever going to own a beach house in Maine. She told herself one day to get a grip; beach houses cost millions of dollars. It was, however, realistic to think she could own a cabin on a lake in Minnesota. After all, lots of people did. Minnesota was the land of 10,000-plus lakes, and she felt sure there was a place for her on one of them. Sophie was a goal-setter. With the arrival of each new calendar year, she dismissed making resolutions. Instead, she held a retreat for herself around February or March, and set both long and short-term personal and professional goals. She considered six-months-to-a-year to be a reasonable time frame for accomplishing many of her short-term goals. The time span for long-term goals was often left open-ended, allowing for realistic expectations. Never short on motivation, she met with ongoing success. With each goal met, she experienced tremendous satisfaction in being able to cross them off the list. Buying the cottage had been one of her long-term goals. She looked at lake property for five years before hearing about a piece of property

The Narrow Gate

for sale on a wonderful sand bottom lake in neighboring southeastern Minnesota. A friend saw the ad in the newspaper and called to tell her about it. The conversation they had was still clear in her mind, *"I wouldn't delay getting in touch with the realtor, Sophie. I rarely see anything for sale on Swan Lake. I think the property will move quickly."* A compelling feeling had come over Sophie, leading her to think this was very likely the right fit she had been waiting for. She immediately placed a call and set up an appointment with the realtor for the very next day.

It was a warm afternoon that late August when she drove out to the country to look at it. The Goldenrod was in bloom. The hillsides revealed just a hint of the fall colors to come. She enjoyed taking the day off and driving through the small rural towns plotted among the endless rolling hills. She caught her breath at the first glimpse of the cozy, seasonal structure as she rounded the curve and turned onto Olde Lake Bottom

Road. The narrow, little country lane meandered through the wooded area dotted with older, two-story cabins. The "for sale" sign read: seventy-five foot lot. For sale by owner. It was a one-story wooden structure, serenely nestled among tall Scotch pine and clusters of birch trees. The beautiful sandy beach was just a few feet from the yard. It was unassuming, but absolutely charming. She fell in love with it the moment she saw it and purchased it immediately.

For the past ten years, she sought out family and hired locals for the help needed to lovingly and tirelessly toil at remodeling and making upgrades. Dark green, wooden shutters were added around the outside windows, giving it a cozy feeling. A three-season wraparound porch, added five years ago, completed the look she desired, as well as the additional sleeping space needed for guests. A shale stone patio and a half circle pergola were her latest additions. The delicate pink New Dawn roses planted symmetrically on each side of the pergola

The Narrow Gate

were thriving, quickly making their way to their final destination atop the structure.

Improvements to the lot were made as well. The borders of her lot were landscaped and enhanced with fresh, fertile dirt in which she planted an assortment of old-fashioned Ragusa rose bushes, lilacs, hydrangeas, and peonies. She took great pride and joy in designing a lavish flower garden in the backyard that included a wide variety of perennial hollyhocks, lilies, daisies, flox, gaillardia, foxglove, iris, poppies, rhubarb, and herbs. A white, arched trellis made of lattice stood front and center amid it all. It provided a framework for the indescribably beautiful lemon chiffon clematis that would soon be covered with blossoms as it climbed its way up both sides, encircling the trellis in the coming weeks. Each June, it would begin to burst forth with an abundance of blossoms and thrive well into August. An explosion of color throughout the yard awaited her as each summer progressed.

Recalling the history of it all now as she continued to drive up the hill, she cautiously looked forward to it, hoping she would still be alive to enjoy it another season.

Her neighbors called her the garden guru. When Sophie was out working in her yard, they often interrupted their walks to saunter around and compliment her on how pretty it all looked and to inquire about what was new in her garden.

Not all, but many of her neighbors were elderly and had spent their summers as youngsters on the lake. As Sophie got to know them over the years, they shared with her tales of growing up on the banks of Swan Lake. They told her of the families that owned each of the cottages and the changes brought when eventually urban sprawl turned rustic resorts into luxurious spas and lakeside restaurants along the south shore. Sophie had been intrigued and especially touched by the story of the newlyweds who, just after the end of WWII, moved into the big brown Tudor at the end of the lane.

"The bride was a southern belle, used to lavish parties and extravaganzas at her home in the heart of Alabama." She could hear her neighbor, Ike, telling her the story in her mind. *"The groom had been a soldier in the Pacific. After a whirlwind wedding, they settled in at the cottage. But after a while, the adjustment to the weeks of isolation and loneliness were too much for the young bride. She set out one day in their small fishing boat towards the other side of the lake. Do you know, she was never heard from again? The boat was found adrift, and the devastated groom was inconsolable and unable to go on without her. No one knows why she did that. The cottage was boarded up until after the death of the groom many years later. Then, eventually, it was sold by the heirs. A retired art professor from Wisconsin and his wife purchased it. They, as well as other residents on Olde Lake Bottom Road, live in their cottages throughout the*

summer, retreating to winter homes in Florida or Arizona for the harsh winter months."

Some of her neighbors were no longer able to garden for themselves. As her garden needed thinning out, Sophie loaded up the two-wheel garden cart with her thinnings and transplanted them to add color and enjoyment to her neighbor's walkways, yards, and barren garden plots. They showed their appreciation and reciprocated with homemade goodies and jams and jellies made from locally grown berries.

She spent countless pleasurable hours observing finch, wrens, hummingbirds, orioles, swallows, and endless waterfowl including the Common Loon, Minnesota's state bird. Friends and family were regular visitors and overnight guests. Sadie's children, Seth, Sydney, and Christian, adored spending weekends—and most of their summer vacations while they were growing up—on Swan Lake catching turtles, fishing, and enjoying lazy summer days on the beach. Just then, she replayed a scene of the four of them playing in the sand. *All of a sudden, the sand began to move. We all got a little closer to see what was going on. Before we knew it, six adorable little turtles were scratching their way out of their eggs and scampering across the sand. The kids got so busy naming each of them. It was such a thrill for all of us to be a part of that. It gave me so much pleasure to share my cozy cottage with all of them. It's my absolute favorite place in the world to be.*

Being involved in solving and writing about horrendous crimes took its toll at times, and she often recharged and healed her wounded soul by spending quiet, carefree time there. She knew it was the place for her to be now. Never one to avoid a problem, she felt she must start the process of searching her soul and coming to terms with the dramatic situation in which she found herself. The drive would give her time to start.

SOPHIE

(Evaluating Her Life)

As she pulled into her driveway, she didn't bother to open the garage door, knowing she wouldn't be long. There was very little she needed to pack. She always left a good supply of clothes and personal items at the cottage. She wanted to change into something more comfortable for the drive, close up the windows, scan the refrigerator for perishables she would need to take with her, and pick up her cat, Rhubarb. Within twenty minutes, she was back in the car heading west towards the highway. Rhubarb was used to the ride, so she promptly curled up on her makeshift bed on the floor of the backseat and went to sleep. Many of the weekday commuters wouldn't be getting off work for another hour, so traffic was light, and she made good time once she left Havendale.

Settling in, she turned her thoughts inward. She was a deeply spiritual person, and she knew that's what would sustain her and get her through this. Neither death nor dying frightened her. She had long ago come to terms with that as the natural order of life, and through her work and in her personal life, she had seen more than her share of death. Alone now with her thoughts and feelings, Sophie recalled those closest to her lost to death. *Losing grandpa Stangler was especially hard. He's been gone seventeen years, and I still think of him daily and miss him terribly. Cancer stealing away my dear friend and coworker, Peggy, at the tender age of twenty-nine was devastating. I had just gotten the job at the Daily after graduating from college, and despite the slight age difference between us, Peggy suggested we share her two bedroom apartment. We soon found we had a lot in common besides the paper, and our friendship grew quickly. What started out as skin cancer metastasized and went to her brain. She died on my twenty-fourth birthday. Lana, Phil, Charlotte, Rachel...all of them gone. Rachel, oh, dear Rachel. How could her husband shoot her while she was washing the kitchen floor in their home? I know things had rapidly deteriorated between them after the birth of their third child because of his drinking. She made the mistake of verbally threatening to take the children and leave him. He just couldn't let that happen, so he took her life. Lana, Phil, and Charlotte, they all died within the past three years from different forms of cancer. I miss them all.*

Despite the sad thoughts, Sophie was not in a woe-is-me, why-me, kind of mood. *Thank you, Lord, for the blessing of being able to share my life with them in the time we had together. I ask you now for the wisdom and guidance to know your will for the remaining days of my life on this earth.*

As she drove on, she began reviewing and evaluating her life. *Well, I can take comfort in knowing I've made a good life for myself. I've gone through different life stages over the years, but I think I've remained open to life and learning.*

There's no major love interest in my life right now, although there certainly have been boyfriends over the years. Will, you were the one I would have said yes to, but you never asked me to marry you. Oh well, marrying you probably would have ended in disaster anyway. I don't think your mother liked me. I sure was dejected and hurt at the time though. I know I drowned myself in my work after that, but it enabled me to get over you and go on with my life.

Do I regret not having children? I still feel so strongly children belong and are better off in a marriage. Not all marriages last, and not all marriages provide good environments for children. Being single though, I just couldn't bring a child in to the world to be raised without the father being intimately involved in its life. That's a huge void for a child to deal with for their entire life. I know of cases where the father has come into the child's life later, but it seems there are always residual effects from the initial rejection. No, I don't regret not having children of my own. I'm so blessed to have Sadie's children in my life. I love them so much.

I had so many opportunities to travel in my younger days. All of the road trips to most of the fifty states and my several trips to Europe to visit Quinn as she moved around were so enjoyable. Let me think, can I still identify the few states I haven't visited? Is it five...the Carolinas, the Virginias, and Mississippi? Those trips were wonderful opportunities to learn about the food, culture, and people unique to those areas. I was especially blessed and I am so grateful for the opportunity to travel to the Holy Land with Sadie and Mom four years ago. I know I've always enjoyed traveling immensely, but I don't feel a desire to pack my bags now and travel off to any unseen destinations.

The fabulous educational opportunities I've had that allowed me to earn my bachelors and later, my master's degree were tremendous blessings, too.

Smiling, her thoughts focused on the people who had been instrumental in guiding her, teaching her, and supporting her along the way.

I've worked hard and done well in my career. My work has allowed me to have all I've needed and more. I've enjoyed tremendous personal fulfillment and satisfaction from my work. I guess it was because of the way I was raised that I've always chosen to live below my financial means. I'm thankful I'm not saddled with debt or money problems. By earthly standards, I suppose I'm successful, although I really have always wanted to hold myself to a higher standard than earthly measures.

The decades have brought personal change and growth, and I feel confident I've reached a point where I've matured and grown deep. My life has real meaning and purpose. I know my talents and gifts, and I've tried to use them to serve and be a blessing to others. I try to live my life in a way that encourages others and enhances their lives, and I want to continue doing so as long as I can.

The plot from a novel she read long ago suddenly entered her train of thought. The main character knew he was dying, so he drafted a list of things to do and places to go before time ran out. Clearly, that wasn't the way she wanted to use her remaining time. She asked herself aloud, "Why would I leave the people I love so much? No, my life is filled with wonderful, loving people who truly mean something to me...who enhance my life, and I need them near me. My soul will journey soon enough."

Then, surprisingly, she realized the blessing of her diagnosis. Images of making travel plans and packing up suitcases as if she were departing on a journey morphed into thoughts of making plans and arrangements to ready her soul for what she believed would be the trip of a lifetime. The similarities impressed upon her the blessing she had received with the forewarning of the storm to come so that she could ready herself. *On the one hand,* she thought, *I'm ready to meet my Creator. As a believer, at times, I have longed to be with Christ. On the other hand, I know I'm not ready in terms of having done it right here on earth. I'm humbled thinking about these things. I can't imagine any believers ever feeling they're in good standing with God in terms of worthiness. It's one thing for me to settle my earthly estate. I can get ready for that, but it's quite another to be thinking of closing out the account, so-to-speak, and settling my eternal estate.*

We are all dying, she thought. *So maybe we should all be living each day as if we were dying. In the end, our lives are the accumulation of our individual days that turn into the weeks, months, and years we are given on this earth. Capturing and really living each day to the fullest will be the essence of living for me. Each day I get is a gift.* The visual of recharging a battery flashed before her. *Am I resigned or remorseful that I can't plug in a day at the end of the day to recharge it, bringing it back to life again? When it's done, it's gone. I need to be sure to treat each day as the gift it really is.* She then readily recited aloud to herself; "This is the day which the Lord hath made; I will rejoice and be glad in it." She breathed deeply then continued her thought. *I've got some major work ahead of me. I can see I will need to start by making time tonight to write out affirmations for preserving the joy in my heart so I don't lose it in the challenges ahead. One thing I'm sure of, God does not want me to live my remaining days bathed in apprehension and doubt.*

What do I want from each day? I know I want and will definitely need deeper faith to guide me. I want to work on being more loving towards others. Peace, I hope for not only peace of mind and heart, but also a deeper peace in my relationships with others.

These tenants will guide me as I go forward and live out the rest of my life. There will be no big changes in my day-to-day life, just these subtle changes in me, in the way I notice and appreciate others and the world around me.

She recited aloud, "Deeper faith, more loving towards others, and peace. Deeper faith, more loving towards others, and peace..."

Her spirit was buoyed by these thoughts. A certain calm came over her, for which she was grateful, because she knew she was most likely in for the rollercoaster ride of her life as things progressed in the coming months.

Let's take it one day at a time, Sophie Beth. You know where your strength lies. Turn your eyes to Him, and just have faith.

RHUBARB
(Little Orphan)

Just then, the sound of a soft meow brought her out of her thoughts. She turned to find Rhubarb straddling the backseat and the arm rest between her and the passenger seat. "Did you have a good nap? We're almost there, baby," she said fondly.

With a smile Sophie recalled, *It was about three years ago. Rhubarb, as a small kitten, wandered into the garden and cowered under the rhubarb leaves during a severe late afternoon rainstorm. The sound of her forlorn cries carried into the cabin as I stood in the kitchen looking out through the ornate, multicolored screen door. I tried to dismiss them,* *but her cries tugged at my heart to the point where I knew without hesitation I had to rescue her. I can remember how the thunder boomed as if it were just yesterday. The crackling lightening lit up the back yard like a 4th of July fireworks display as I donned my rain boots and umbrella and headed outside. It was a drenching downpour. The two of us were soaked to the bone when I returned to the cottage.*

I remember how caringly I wiped her down to dry her off. I thought she was going to eat me out of house and home! That was one of the longest nights of my life. It had to have been about nine o'clock in the evening when I realized the trembling and constant meowing were not because my little guest was still cold, but because she was frightened. So like a mother soothing her newborn, I opened a towel and wrapped her in it. Oh, how I held her in my arms, rocking and cooing to her until she herself was exhausted. Unable to take any more, I brought her to bed with me, but neither of us slept much. I think it was around four o'clock in the morning that she finally settled down and dozed off. I, too, fell into a deep sleep.

The next day went better. She had stopped shaking, and she was able to quiet herself down. I remember the exact minute I took to calling her Rhubarb. That was when I found myself becoming attached to the little orphan. The inquiries I made around the neighborhood and posting flyers with Rhubarb's picture were unsuccessful in producing her owner. No one seemed to know anything about her. I took her back to Havendale for the week and returned to the cottage the next weekend thinking I would hear something. Still no one claimed her. Before long, two weeks had passed without anyone coming forth to identify her as theirs. It was then I decided it was time to make her a permanent member of my family.

We've been loving and faithful companions ever since, and Rhubarb has certainly thrived under my care. Like most young cats, she's spirited and so full of pep! Unless I want to find them strewn all over the floor again, I've got to be more careful about placing the paper towel rolls in the oven for safekeeping while I'm gone. My stockings, too, need to be carried off to the laundry basket immediately after removing my shoes unless I want to find them in shreds again. She's such a pretty girl with impeccable hygiene, always keeping her coal-black coat immaculate and shiny. Her four white paws are always snow-white. I swear she has an almost human-like intelligence!"

It hadn't happened often, but occasionally in the past on an overcast gloomy Monday morning, Sophie had a hard time rousing from bed. Almost human-like, Rhubarb had grown to know her routine and knew when she overslept. Like clockwork, Rhubarb jumped up on the bed, forcefully making her way under the covers to bite Sophie's toes! Those sharp, prickly teeth piercing her tender skin made Sophie spring to life faster than a mousetrap activated by an unsuspecting scavenger following the scent of peanut butter.

In spite of the aggravation, I adore her. I can't imagine life without her. That reminds me, I need to start thinking about making sure Rhubarb is well taken care of after I'm gone.

Up ahead, Sophie could see the turn-off leading to the cottages. She felt a sense of coming home. The picturesque Victorian home she owned in Havendale suited her well, but the cottage was where she left her heart. Anticipating the weekend momentarily put a blissful smile on her face.

"We're here, Rhubarb," she said softly. Within a short time, she had carried everything into the cottage and gotten settled. A slight hunger pang reminded her that according to the clock, it was time to eat something. She brushed it aside thinking she couldn't possibly be hungry after the big lunch she had eaten just a few hours ago. Rhubarb meowed and rubbed against her leg then looked up at Sophie with a look that said she wanted attention.

"Ok, girl. Let's go outside for some fresh air. We'll check on the neighbors, and let them know we're here. After that, I've got some eternal estate planning to think about!"

MOLLY

(Marcus, Where Are You?)

"Hi, sweetie! Sorry I'm late," she called out to Marcus as she entered the house, struggling with an overflowing bag of groceries. She anticipated he was probably tired after an exhausting fifty-hour workweek and expected to find him relaxing just off the kitchen in the den. "I got hung up at the doctor's office," she continued as she headed towards the counter. "Everything's great with the baby. The doctor says we're right on schedule, hon. There was an emergency earlier in the day, so her schedule got messed up. I had to wait two hours before I could even get in to see her." Setting the groceries

The Narrow Gate

down and turning to walk towards the den, she queried, "Marcus, hon, could you come out here? I stopped at the market, and I could use a little help unloading the rest of the groceries from the car. Honey, are you here?" *That's odd*, she thought as she reached the den and saw that he was nowhere in sight. *I wonder if he's in the garage or the backyard.* She headed towards the garage. *I'm sure I'll meet him coming in to answer my calls.* As she approached the garage, she could see through the window his car wasn't there. A quick check of the yard and then her cell phone revealed he wasn't home, and he hadn't called.

It wasn't like him to run late, and she began to wonder, *Did he mention anything earlier in the week about something special going on today that I've forgotten about?* Pregnancy did strange things, not only to one's body, but also the mind. She had been somewhat forgetful recently. Nothing came to mind, so she brushed it off and continued to unload the car. Thirty minutes later the groceries had been put away, and she had changed clothes. Standing in the kitchen looking out the window, she felt perplexed. There was still no sign of him or any word from him. It was now a few minutes before seven o'clock, and the feelings of concern that had crept in were mingling with feelings of doubt and confusion. Pulling the phone out of her purse, she hit speed dial. After four rings, she heard the prerecorded message, "You have reached the voice mailbox of Marcus Crandall. Please leave your name, telephone number, and a brief message. Your call will be returned as soon as possible."

I don't want to embarrass myself by letting him know I've forgotten if he told me about a special event. Trying hard to speak casually, in a matter-of-fact manner, she began, "Marcus, this is Molly. Honey, it's seven o'clock, and I'm wondering how much longer you're going to be. Call me. I love you babe."

I hope the concern I'm feeling didn't come through in my voice. He would think I'm being silly. Laying down the phone, she wasn't sure what to do. She didn't want to overreact, but this was so out of character for him.

On his own, he is never late. I'm the one who can be challenged by time occasionally and make him late, she mused. She began to reminisce. *Early in our relationship he was so patient with me whenever I lost track of time or over-scheduled myself. I kept him waiting sometimes for hours. It's the little things that can drive a wedge between two people, but wisely, Marcus has always been patient with me. Gently, he provided the structure I needed, and I learned to organize my time better. I've grown in other, bigger ways, too, because of him and the influence and wisdom he lovingly brings to my life.* Different, yet so much alike, she felt sweet satisfaction as she thought of him now. *I love you so much, Marcus.*

From the day they met on a blind date, set up by their two best friends, she knew she had found her soulmate. They were married after a brief, six-month courtship. She was attracted to him immediately, and it wasn't just because of his beautiful, six-foot-tall, athletic body and dark good looks. They were both accountants with similar career goals. Growing up with similar backgrounds, they shared family values, political views, and temperaments. Beyond those things, Molly had always felt so comfortable with Marcus. *I can talk to him about anything. He always seems to say the right things with genuine honesty and sincerity. He is uniquely sensitive to my feelings. I always count on him for understanding and support. I love his sense of humor. He helps me lighten up and see things in a different light. You've never let me down, honey. You're one of the most honest people I know. I can't think of anyone I respect more.*

Deep in thoughts of what a phenomenal father he would be, she was startled as her thoughts suddenly took a turn. *If something awful has happened to him, would I sense it? Is there that kind of bond between us?* The answer to her question came, strangely, moments later when a horrifying chill permeated her entire body. She knew, without knowing, that something was terribly wrong. With trembling hands, she reached for the phone and nervously placed a call to Marcus' coworker, Si Hanson. After several rings, his automated voice message began to play, and she broke down and sobbed uncontrollably. Utter devastation came over her as she made her way to the table and struggled to pull out a chair. *Stop! You're not doing Marcus any good by falling apart like this,* she thought as she sat down. *I've got to get control of myself.*

Slowly, she began to pull herself together and was able to make the decision to drive over to his office. Making her way to the sink, she began splashing cold water on her face. Her hands continued to shake, but she welcomed a minute sense of composure. As she dried her face and turned to reach for her purse, the phone rang. Almost frantically, she grabbed it. Without looking to see who was calling, she heard herself answer in a voice filled with anguish, "Marcus, is that you?"

A female voice asked, "Are you the lady of the house?"

Feelings of fear and torment threatened to paralyze her.

Full of hesitation, Molly replied, "Who, who is this?"

"Ma'am, we're conducting a poll for the..."

On the verge of tears again, she somehow managed to hold it together as she disconnected the phone and bolted for the door.

PARK

(A Dead Body)

*S*itting at his computer, wrapping up a report of the day's events, Havendale police detective, Parker Sims, answered the call on line one. He listened as Officer Lucie Tate tried her best to relay what little of the message she understood from a distraught male. "He said he was calling in to report a dead body. He's still on the line, Park. I'll put him through to you."

Within seconds, Park could hear the all-too-familiar breathlessness and panic coming over the line. The disturbed voice of an unwitting citizen experiencing the grizzly scene of an accident rang in his ear.

Park

"Whoa! Slow down, man; try to calm down. This is Detective Sims. I'm here to help you. Take a few deep breaths; then we'll talk."

After a pause, the man proceeded to speak with less urgency, "My name is Garrett Lindquist. I've just come upon a dead body at the bottom of the south hill near Coven's Corner. I'm out jogging. I happened to look off to my left, and I saw something. It looked like a heap of something sort of sticking out by a clump of trees. I stopped and went over to check it out and got the scare of a lifetime! I've never been so scared. It's a man. I'm sure he's dead. Hurry, hurry and get here."

Park had already put in a ten hour workday. Upon hearing the startling news, he didn't hesitate to lunge out of his chair as he reached for his car keys and dashed out the door. Reaching the scene of the incident, his eyes scanned the site for Garrett. His attention was drawn to a frail-looking man with a pasty white pallor.

The man was standing on the curb flailing his arms. As Park exited the vehicle and began walking toward him, he could see how obviously shaken the man was.

"Mr. Lindquist? I'm Detective Park Sims," he stated as he extended his hand.

"Yes, I am Garrett Lindquist," he replied as he also extended his hand in exchange.

"Thank you for calling. I need you to show me the body. Did you touch anything or move anything at the scene of the body?"

"No I didn't touch anything. I can't go back over there." He said nervously as he pointed across the street. He then added, "It's straight over there, hidden by that cluster of pine trees. He's face up. I can't look at his face, again. His eyes are open."

Park thought the man was close to vomiting. "You don't look well. Sit down here on the curb for a while. I'll go over there and check things out."

Kneeling down and examining the body for a pulse, Park immediately determined the man was dead. He began visually examining the scene. He called in the usual team of resources before turning his attention back to Garrett to interview him in more detail. The police arrived and began to cordon off the area and document the scene with pictures. Forensics personnel and Gus Thompson, the coroner, arrived on the scene a short time later. Gus called out, "What have you got, Park, a jumper?"

Standing over the body, Park slowly shook his head as he said, "I don't think so, Gus." Park cast his glance upwards toward the top of the tree line to the barely visible balcony where Marcus had stood earlier that day and pointed for Gus to do the same. "Do you see that balcony? If our victim jumped from there, he would have landed face down. I've interviewed the man who called in the incident. He said he didn't touch the body. Unless someone else was here and moved it, I'd say there's a good chance we could have a murder on our hands."

By the look on Gus' face, Park could tell he had clearly caught him off guard. With that, Gus immediately rolled up his sleeves and went right to work.

Murder wasn't a daily occurrence in the small hamlet of Havendale like it was in large metropolitan areas. As Park thought about it, he supposed the last murder investigation he conducted in his sleepy little town of twenty-thousand inhabitants was a good eight to ten years ago. Still, his twenty years of experience as a police officer and seven years as a detective enabled him to quickly determine that Garrett's recounting of how he came upon the body was legitimate. The statements he made, his demeanor, and his body language all led Park to believe he was not culpable of any crime toward the victim. Park quickly ruled him out as a suspect. Garrett was still visibly shaken. Since he had just happened upon the body after the fact, rather than actually seeing anything going down, Park didn't need him at the scene anymore.

"Officer, it isn't necessary for Mr. Lindquist to stay here any longer.

Take him to the station to get his statement. He'll be free to go after that. You'd better drive him home."

Shadows of twilight began creeping in, and it was a welcome relief for Garrett to be able to leave the scene.

When the body was ready to be released, Gus loaded it up for the trip to the morgue where he would conduct the autopsy. "I'll give you a call, Park, when I've got the results," Gus shouted out the window as he drove away.

Park, too, got in his car and headed back to the station with Marcus' personal effects, leaving the rest of the team at the site.

At the station, he briefly shared the personal identity of the victim with Lucie. "We were able to I.D. the victim by his driver's license. His name is Marcus Crandall." Park handed the personal effects over to her. It was her job to catalog the victim's belongings and begin the search for the next-of-kin. Walking to his office, Park was struck with feelings of loss and sadness. The wedding ring on Marcus' left hand revealed the knowledge that somewhere out there was a young widow. He speculated. *Perhaps there are small children, too, who will never again see their father.* Shaking his head and sighing deeply, he sat down to begin his initial incident report. Presently unaware of the swift and evil strike, which was responsible for snuffing out the fiery will to live that had burned in Marcus Crandall, a fire began to burn in him. It was fueled by a fierce determination to find out what happened to Marcus Crandall.

MOLLY

(My Husband Is Missing!)

As Molly maneuvered her car into the parking lot surrounding the courthouse, the ample light from both the headlights and the street lamps rested on the lone car in front of her. Not knowing what to make of finding Marcus' car here at work and the building completely dark, she felt little relief. She was no longer on the verge of panic, but the urgent feeling that something was terribly wrong had not left her. *If he's still here at the office, why hasn't he returned my call?* Once again, she dialed his number and waited for him to answer. Un-assuaged at the sound of his voicemail message, she swallowed hard. She hesitated for just a moment. Then in a timid, quivering voice, she said, "Marcus, it's Molly again. Honey, I'm outside in the parking lot. If you can hear me, please pick up the phone. I need to talk to you." The silence on the other end of the line was excruciating.

In a moment of utter desperation and helplessness, she rapidly put the car in gear. The car careened and squealed out of the parking lot as she headed toward the police station. Her thoughts filled her with apprehension as she raced down the south hill. *What will I say? With nothing to go on but my feelings, how will I convince the police that something truly is amiss? How will I get them to understand they need to take me seriously?* In her condition, it took considerable effort to exit the car and run straight for Lucie's desk as she entered the station. "My husband is missing." She shouted frantically. "I know something awful has happened to him. Please, you have to believe me. His car is in the parking lot at work, but he's not there and he's not answering my calls."

Molly

As Lucie looked up, there was no mistaking the look of torment on Molly's face. Calmly, Lucie responded by getting up and pulling out a chair so Molly could sit across from her. "I can see you are very upset, and I'll do what I can to help you. Try to calm down, dear, so you can tell me everything. My name is Lucie Tate. What is your name?"

"Thank you. My name is Molly Crandall."

Lucie instantly recognized the name, Crandall, as the surname of the deceased male in Park's new investigation. "Wait here," she said reassuringly. "I'm going to get Detective Sims. You'll need to talk directly to him."

Had Molly known Marcus' fate at that time, the slight sense of hope she began to feel would have been dashed in an instant, leaving her stunned and filled with pain. Instead, she felt relieved, even hopeful, upon hearing she was going to be able to talk to a detective.

Lucie returned with Park at her side. "Mrs. Crandall, this is Detective

The Narrow Gate

Park Sims. Park, meet Mrs. Molly Crandall."

Park immediately noticed her condition and her state of agitation. He motioned for Lucie to get her some water.

"Mrs. Crandall, I'd like you to come to my office where we can talk about your husband," he said somberly. Unbeknownst to her, as she struggled to get her balance and rise out of the chair, he dreaded the awful task of informing her of her husband's demise. He was worried about how the news might affect her pregnancy. He extended his arm to support her. As the two of them walked arm-and-arm toward his office, Lucie reached out to her with a glass of water and followed along behind them. She gently closed the door behind her.

The news of the colossal loss of her dear Marcus proved to be too much. Devastated and overcome by grief, she was rushed to the Havendale Community Hospital by ambulance, with a worried Lucie right by her side.

SADIE

(A Stranger In Need)

*A*s the sun rose silently in the sky ushering in a new day, Sadie bound out of bed feeling refreshed and alert. She had enjoyed a peaceful night's sleep. Sydney's surprise weekend visit was a welcome distraction, taking her mind off the uneasy feeling she had experienced the night before.

She was scheduled to volunteer at the hospital later today. Holding the babies, snuggling with the older children while reading aloud to them, and spending the rest of the day with Sydney making preliminary wedding plans filled her with anticipation. As she busied herself with household chores, her mood was cheerful. Her thoughts were consumed with the newness of the news that her little girl was getting married in approximately seven months. She and Ted loved Michael, and she felt peaceful knowing Sydney would have a warm and loving marriage. As a mother, it was a special blessing and meant so much to her knowing her little girl had chosen a wonderful man to be her partner in life.

The time passed quickly. Soon, she found herself in the car heading towards the hospital. The parking lot was unusually full, forcing her to park on the west side and enter the building through a different entrance than usual. As she entered the hallway, she immediately heard the mournful cries of a deeply distressed female. Her charitable heart went out to the poor soul, and she instinctively headed in the direction of the devastating sounds. Just around the corner, she gently tapped on the door to room #203. A deeply troubled Molly Crandall was beside herself with grief as she sat up in bed. Seeing her there all alone tugged at Sadie's heart, and she flew to her bedside, wrapping her caring arms around her and gently rocking her upper body from side-to-side. She soothingly began stroking Molly's hair. Holding her close, she closed her eyes and softly prayed aloud, "God please intercede in this precious woman's life. Bring her peace and comfort so she will know the warmth of your love." Time seemed to stand still as they continued to be joined together. Then, slowly, Molly was able to move out of the embrace.

"Hello, I'm Sadie, one of the volunteers in the pediatric ward."

"I'm Molly. I've just found out that my husband is dead. He went to work yesterday, and didn't come home."

Sadie sat mutely horrified as Molly struggled to continue sharing some of the details. It was very difficult for her to talk about it. "We won't know the official cause of death until the autopsy report, but I'm afraid Detective Sims thinks it's suicide. There is no way Marcus would do that. We were crazy about each other. I'm having a c-section on May 22. It's our first baby, and he was over the moon with excitement. We've been trying for seven years. We were both so happy. I just know he didn't jump. He had too much to live for."

Before Sadie could respond, Molly broke down and began crying hysterically, again.

The nurse, who had been monitoring her closely, reentered the room to administer a light sedative that would not hurt the baby, and take her blood pressure. Sadie took her other hand, and in a soft caring voice, she assured her with the words, "I'll be right here, Molly, until you fall asleep. I'll leave you to rest, but I promise I'll return later."

Before too long, Molly drifted off to sleep. Sadie quietly slipped out of the room. Feeling troubled and heartsick as she entered the elevator that transported her to the next floor, she was moved to take on the responsibility to do all she could to help Molly.

When the elevator doors opened, Sadie stepped onto the pediatric ward where she glanced at her watch and learned she had missed her story hour with the kids. Paige Rogers, the hospital's very efficient volunteer coordinator, always had a back-up plan. It was safe to assume someone else covered for her. She couldn't help feeling some remorse in letting the kids down by not being there today. She prided herself on the commitment she made upon initially volunteering. She was reliable and consistent in that commitment although she had no regrets about making time for Molly.

Heading for the sitting area, she reached for her cell phone and hit speed dial. Sophie answered on the second ring, and listened in rapt silence as Sadie proceeded to relay the details of her morning with Molly. Sophie, too, was touched and deeply moved by the tragedy. Immense pride over the warmth and compassion Sadie was showing to Molly swelled within her. A compulsion to express her feelings to Sadie came over her.

"You're a wonderfully caring, loving person, Sadie Grace. I'm so proud of you for reaching out to her the way you did. You responded in a very giving way to a stranger in desperate need, and I love you for it. If everything she told you is true, she's right. Suicide doesn't make sense. It's premature though, at this point, to second-guess Park. He really has to wait for the autopsy report before addressing the official cause of death with her. If anything suspicious turns up, he'll want me to be part of the investigation. You know I'll do everything I can to help her. Understandably, she's giving in to hysteria. For now, help her contact friends and family. She's going to need a lot of support."

"I will. Sophie, as heartbreaking as Molly's situation is, I have to say, I'm filled with relief that it's not someone in our own family that's going through a crisis."

Stunned, Sophie inquired, "What are you talking about?"

"I didn't say anything to you yesterday, but we can talk about it now. The night before last, I had some kind of premonition or warning of an impending disaster or crisis. Sophie, the feeling was so totally overwhelming; it woke me up. I was absolutely filled with dread, and I wasn't able to go back to sleep. I couldn't identify what it all meant at the time. I just had this overwhelming feeling something horrible was going to happen. Well, now, I think it was a forewarning of the death of Molly's husband. I feel a little guilty for saying this, but I am so relieved. What do you think?"

"Well I, I think that's a natural reaction, Sadie," she stammered.

"Let's talk about it another time."

A brief exchange about Sydney's engagement followed before the conversation ended. Sophie was shaken by the news of Sadie's uncanny insight. The thought of facing Sadie and confirming the news of a very real family disaster made her tremble. Sadie, on the other hand, was filled with a renewed sense of well-being. She was soon heading off in the direction of the children's ward to begin a round of brief visits with the children individually in their rooms. As she gently opened the door and entered room #320, six-month-old Toby Bennett greeted her with a million dollar smile that tickled her very soul. His distraught mother was holding him in her arms, but she willingly passed him off to Sadie. She held out her arms and embraced him, nuzzling nose-to-nose.

Toby was awaiting heart surgery to correct an aortic stenosis, just one of many challenges he had faced since suffering a stroke at birth. His young parents were absolutely devoted to him and were working hard along with various therapists to give him all the at-home care he needed to overcome the devastating effects of the stroke. The stenosis was a separate issue, and neither of them expected surgery to be necessary at this time of his life.

Sadie looked up and gave them both a warm smile. "How are the two of you doing today?" The response she got was a tearful, unintelligible cry for reassurance from Ava Bennett. She gently handed Toby over to his anxious father and wrapped her arms around Ava. With a giving spirit in her heart, she thought, *I will definitely be changing my plans with Sydney in order to spend as much time as needed with this precious little family and Molly today.*

SOPHIE

(Murder In Havendale)

An early afternoon sun glistened on Swan Lake as Sophie tried to relax outside on the patio. It was a beautiful day with a gentle northwest breeze coming across the lake. Surrounded by the buzz of motors, she sat watching an endless parade of boats and jet skis whiz by. She felt conflicted and filled with uneasiness since her conversation with Sadie. She was trying to put it into perspective. There would be an appropriate time, and she would tell Sadie about her tumor at that time. She was also just very happy to be alive. More keenly aware that the clock of life was ticking, she softly whispered, "Day two. Please help me live it in service to you, Lord."

Her thoughts had also periodically returned to Marcus and Molly Crandall. As she thought of them now, she impulsively locked up the cottage, tucked Rhubarb in the car, and headed back to Havendale. She quickly deposited Rhubarb at home and filled her food and water dish before heading to the police station.

Lucie was on duty. They smiled warmly at each other as Sophie entered the station. Over the years they had worked many cases together, and Sophie held her in high esteem for the gift she had of balancing extremely efficient skills with warmth and sensitivity towards victim's family members. Lucie knew immediately why Sophie was there and what she would need. "I had a hunch you would be in soon," Lucie stated as she efficiently retrieved Marcus' personal effects. She promptly laid out the photos of the scene.

"You're the best, Lucie. Thank you. I just couldn't stay away." Sophie said as she began to study the photos.

The Narrow Gate

As the two of them stood pouring over the pictures, Lucie shared her belief that this was not a suicide. "I've spoken to his wife, and he had everything to live for. It sounds like they adored each other and were ecstatic about the upcoming birth of their first baby."

"You're right, Lucie, this wasn't suicide. Sadie spoke with his wife, too, at the hospital this morning. She told me the same thing. Look at these marks on his stomach, and here, look at this."

Just then, the phone rang. It was Gus from the coroner's office calling to say he was faxing the results of the autopsy.

Park walked in as Lucie hung up the phone. "What have you got, Stangler, ESP? I haven't even gotten results from Gus, yet."

"Nice to see you, too, Sims," she bantered in return as she turned to look at him. "I've got an inside connection on this one; Sadie's at the hospital with the vic's wife. I think we've got a problem here."

Lucie interrupted their playful exchange by handing Park the fax. As he read silently, the two of them continued to study pictures.

"Yeah," he shook his head as he finished reading, "murder can be a problem." The three of them turned and looked at each other nodding in unanimous agreement as what they had suspected all along was confirmed.

They each found the death of a young man, in the prime of his life with a new baby on the way, hard to acknowledge. To learn that his life was violently taken from him was unnerving. Simultaneously, their forlorn thoughts turned to Molly. Park was the first to break the gloomy silence. "His wife fell apart at the news of his death. We weren't able to get any information from her. Let's go over to the hospital now, Stangler, and hope she can give us something helpful."

It was a welcome sight to see a subdued Molly talking quietly to Sadie as they entered her hospital room. The hysteria that Park had seen in her earlier was gone, replaced with a sadness that seemed to pierce her very soul. Sophie felt a sense of relief that Sadie was still there. Again, she took pride in Sadie as she introduced herself to Molly as Sadie's sister. Compassionately, Park delivered the heart-wrenching news to her. "Mrs. Crandall, I'm so sorry. The death of your husband is a tragic loss. We don't believe your husband's death was a suicide. We also don't believe it was an accident. I'm afraid we suspect someone was responsible for his death. I promise you, we will do everything we can to find out what happened to him. We will make it our top priority to get to the bottom of what happened. We'll need to ask you some questions, and it's important that you give us your full cooperation."

Molly was greatly relieved to hear his death was not ruled a suicide, but horrified to learn her husband was murdered. Although she knew nothing of Marcus' business dealings, she was able to give them enough adequate information about Hyshum and Lester, and Marcus' friends and coworkers, for them to start inquiring.

Sophie and Park immediately set about contacting Dick Lester to obtain access to Marcus' office. The firm didn't observe Saturday hours so they caught up with him by phone at his home. When the three of them met at the courthouse, Dick appeared pale and genuinely distressed.

"I can't believe he's gone. Marcus was an exceptional employee. He was a rising star. I have no doubt there was a senior partnership for him in the future."

They entered the courthouse. Park put in a call to his office for assistance as he headed toward the balcony. Sophie and Dick entered Marcus' office.

"Can you think of anyone who would want to harm him or any reason for anyone to want to see him dead?" Sophie inquired.

"No, no. Marcus was a peacemaker not a trouble maker. He never indicated anything to me about having any trouble with any of his coworkers or clients."

They caught a lucky break. The computer was still on; bearing witness to what Marcus had been working on just prior to his demise. Dick cooperated fully, answering all of Sophie's additional questions and offering further information about employees.

"Let me know if I can do anything more to help you with the investigation," he volunteered. "What about Molly? Has she been notified?"

"Yes, she has been informed of her husband's death. Unfortunately, the news was overwhelming for her. She's in the hospital. I would say she's doing about as well as can be expected. They're keeping a very close eye on her."

"My wife and I will make sure she has everything she needs. We would be very willing to help her make the arrangements for burial if she needs help."

"I'm not sure what she needs, but I'm sure she would appreciate all of your offers to help. She's in room #203."

Park's staff showed up and began a thorough search of the crime scene.

Park and Sophie left separately to begin interviewing Marcus' coworkers. None of them were aware of the situation. Park set out in pursuit of Danny Lockwood. Simon Hanson was first on Sophie's list. As they traveled, they both agonized at the thought of the extremely unpleasant task ahead. Sophie was prompted to focus her thoughts on generating a sense of peace, "I feel calm and peaceful. I feel calm and peaceful." She repeated the affirmation twenty times. It was just one of the ways she engaged in positive self-speak and remained mindful of her thoughts. She was committed to achieving her goals of deeper faith, a more loving affect, and peace in her life.

Glancing out the window of her car as she pulled alongside the curb, Sophie admired the view of Mr. Hanson's stately Queen Ann-style Victorian mansion sitting atop the small hill. Four vivid colors accentuated the architectural details of whimsical fish scale shingles and magnificent carpenter's lace along the edge of the roof. A large porch wrapped itself around the front and one side of the house, with French doors leading into what she envisioned as a parlor or perhaps a music room. Off to the left side of the house, on the second story, was a round room with a Scandinavian-style turret atop the roof. The real estate market in town wasn't as strong as it once was, but she guessed the current market value to be easily a million dollars at least. She found herself wondering, *What kind of money would you need just to maintain a house like this and keep the lights on?*

Stepping onto the porch and lifting the doorknocker on the spoon carved pine door, she heard the muffled sounds of two men arguing. Curious to know who might be in the house, she strolled over to the side of the porch where she observed two very expensive looking vehicles parked in the driveway. She reached in her pocket to retrieve her phone. She snapped a picture of them before going back to rap on the door a second time.

In the time it took for the door to open, she looked about and really noticed what a beautiful warm, spring day it was. It seemed as if the birds were singing just for her. It made her smile, and filled her with a gentle sense of peace as she briefly called to her memory the comforting message she found in Matthew 6:25-27: *"Don't worry about everyday life. Look at the birds and the flowers. Your heavenly Father feeds them and cares for them, and you are far more valuable to Him than they are. Your heavenly Father knows all your needs, and He will give you all you need from day to day if you live for Him and make the Kingdom of God your primary concern."*

The sound of an engine starting pulled her away from her thoughts and made her dart back to the side of the porch. She witnessed one of the vehicles speeding away. Her trained eye caught the license number on the car, and she noted the driver was small in stature with black hair. She didn't recognize him.

Turning back to the man now at the door, she saw he was clearly very agitated. "Mr. Hanson?"

"Yes, I'm Simon Hanson. Call me Si."

"Sophie Stangler, *Minneapolis Daily*. Are you all right? I heard arguing."

"Yes, I know who you are. I recognize you from your picture in the paper. No, no, what you heard was nothing. We weren't really arguing, Ms. Stangler. We were just discussing something, nothing important. We disagreed, that's all. I'm fine."

"You can call me Sophie. I'm afraid I have some bad news for you. Perhaps it would be best if we went inside so you could sit down."

"All right, yes, come in," he said rather abruptly.

Following him into a beautifully restored front parlor, she headed for one of the Victorian loveseats as he motioned for her to sit down. He, too, settled on an expensive looking overstuffed chair. Gazing around, she noticed the original hardwood floors had been exquisitely restored and partially covered with expensive looking Oriental wool rugs. The room was lavishly decorated with a baby grand piano in the corner and down-filled cushions on both of the settees. An extensive and very expensive looking collection of 16th century Majolica adorned the tables and built-in wall units. Rare and unusual pieces in excellent condition were arranged in a pleasingly colorful display. A massive set of pocket doors were slightly pulled out, standing at attention between the room they were in and what looked like a formal dining room.

"What, what's happened?" he asked curtly.

"I'm afraid I'm here to inform you of the death of your coworker, Marcus Crandall."

His response came in a flat, matter-of-fact tone of voice, "Marcus is dead?"

Sophie was not only a well-trained and experienced investigator; she was also an extremely intuitive human being. Her ability to sense things with insight was keen. His unusual

The Narrow Gate

response activated that sensing antennae in her now, and she broke out in goose bumps.

"His office was right across from yours, and I'm hoping you may have heard something or perhaps had a conversation with him in which he may have told you something that would help my investigation. If you don't mind my asking, who were you talking to just now?"

"It's not important, I told you." His response was stiff and brisk.

"Si, I'm investigating the death of a young man in the prime of his life. I need your full cooperation in answering my questions. Let me decide what's important."

"I don't know anything. I can't help you. I'm shocked to hear Marcus is dead."

Unconvinced by the tone of his voice, Sophie pressed on. "Si, I'm going to ask you again. Who was the man you were talking to before he sped off?"

Looking to the ground, he reluctantly gave up the name, "Danny.

Just my friend, Danny, that's all. It was nothing."

"Would that be Danny Lockwood, another coworker from your firm?" she inquired.

"Yes," he answered in a small voice. "We socialize outside of work, and we played golf together earlier this morning. My game was right on, and, well, let me just say I'm afraid he did not go down well in defeat. That's what you overheard us discussing. As I said, it was nothing."

A feeling came over Sophie. She wasn't buying the line she thought he was selling. She continued to question him. "Tell me about your day at work yesterday. Where were you between the hours of eleven and, say, one o'clock in the afternoon?"

"My morning was uneventful. It was just another day at work. I was there until I left the office to meet a client for lunch. His name is Trevor Kline. We dined at the Harbor Bar and Grill. Plenty of people saw me there. I can't help you. I don't know anything."

The Narrow Gate

"What kind of relationship did you have with Marcus?"

"We worked together. That's all. We got along fine. Occasionally, we played a round of golf together. Oh, yes, I remember; he talked about setting up a golf date soon. That was the last thing he said to me. I then left to join Mr. Kline at the Harbor."

"Did you socialize outside of work, other than playing golf together?"

"No, no, we didn't."

Learning of his luncheon with a client around the time of the assumed murder appeared to give him a clear-cut alibi. Things were not always as they seemed, however. He was outmatched by her years of experience at ferreting out details and vital information. Sophie felt certain he was holding back information vital to shining light on what happened to Marcus. She knew this would not be the last conversation she would have with him. He was either unable or unwilling to tell her where Danny was going when he drove off. A quick click on her phone sent a text message

Sophie

to Park, letting him know Danny's license number and that he had been at Si's house.

SOPHIE AND PARK
(Of One Mind)

The following week, Sophie and Park put all their energy into the investigation talking to many other Hyshum and Lester employees and Trevor Kline.

Marcus' coworkers were devastated by his death. Some were numb with grief and unable to report to work. Sophie and Park spent hours meeting with them in their homes asking the questions that revealed their relationships to Marcus and possible motives for murder. All of them expressed genuine respect and admiration for Marcus, leaving no doubt with either Park or Sophie that they were not involved in his death.

Sophie continued to feel a nagging suspicion of Si, even though Mr. Kline had substantiated his alibi.

"It's time for me to pay a second visit to Si," she stated to Park as they walked towards their cars.

"You took the words right out of my mouth, Stangler."

Pausing briefly to look down at the ground, then cocking his head to the side as he looked directly into her eyes, he said, "We make a good team, Sophie."

He quickly cleared his throat and continued in a hurried manner, "I'll make contact with Danny then meet up with you at my office later."

Sophie nodded in agreement and climbed into her car.

Sophie. He called me Sophie. How about that? Huh! We've never worked a murder case together, yet, we seem to be of one mind as we go about it. I guess we do make a good team. It feels good doing this with him. He's such a good man. I wonder what would have happened if we had met thirty years ago! Under the circumstances, it's best not to think about that.

The look of shock on Si's face as he opened the door and saw her standing there was evident to Sophie before he spoke the words, "I'm surprised to see you again. I've already told you everything I know."

"May I come in? I really would like to talk again. There may be something you've remembered, or perhaps you know something you didn't think was worth mentioning the last time we spoke."

Si moved aside to allow Sophie to enter.

Walking over to the side of the room, she ran her fingers across the shelf of a beautiful built-in bookcase.

"I noticed and admired your collection of Majolica the last time I was here. You have some beautiful pieces."

"Yes, I've been collecting for quite some time, and I have some rare pieces that are quite valuable."

Sophie carefully picked up a small rectangular glass box with a lid adorned in a mermaid motif. The aqua and pink coloring were classic majolica, and the piece was in mint condition. As she lifted the lid off and turned it over, she was surprised to find a washboard-like surface. She frowned momentarily as her mind ran through a myriad of thoughts about the purpose of the rough surface. Suddenly, it became clear.

"Ah-ha! It's a match box!"

"Yes, you guessed correctly, but I don't think you came here to admire my collection of Majolica. What can I do for you, Ms. Stangler?"

Sophie set the piece down carefully and turned to face Si.

"I'm hoping you have remembered something about the last time you saw Marcus that may help me determine what happened to him."

Si sighed and shook his head as he responded, "I've told you everything I know. As I said, when I left the office to meet my client for lunch, Marcus was very much alive. I wish I knew something that would help."

"Did you notice anything unusual or different about him that morning?

What was his demeanor? Did he seem upset about anything?"

"No. There was nothing unusual about him. We spoke very briefly before I left."

"Did you see anyone standing around by his office or hear anything unusual at any time that morning?"

"No, I didn't see anyone and nothing seemed out of the ordinary. Marcus was congenial and as I said, we spoke about getting together to play golf. Oh, wait. I just remembered; he did say he had found a glitch in one of his accounts."

"What did you think he meant when he mentioned this glitch?"

"I didn't think anything of it at the time. I just thought he was making casual conversation about his work. Come to think of it now, though, he may have been referring to a mistake he made. He was dealing with accounts in the millions. If he made a mistake that would cost the company a lot of money, that would have been hard for someone like Marcus to live with. I knew him, Ms. Stangler;

he was very conscientious. I can see where being responsible for a loss to the company would drive him to end his life."

"Are you saying you think he committed suicide because he was distraught or in a panic over making a mistake that would have cost the company a large sum of money?"

"No. I'm not saying that. I don't know what happened to Marcus. I'm just speculating because you asked me what I thought he could have meant."

All of her instincts told her this was a desperate attempt on Si's part to deflect suspicion off him, but she responded with feigned interest.

"We don't believe Marcus' death was a suicide, Si, but I'll look into his accounting practices. Thank you for your time."

Clearly looking stunned by what he had just heard, Si reacted loudly, "Wait. Are you saying Marcus was murdered?"

"Yes, we believe that is what happened. If you think of anything that you haven't already mentioned to me, please call me. Here's my card with my direct number. Again, thanks for your time."

Sophie was filled with the overwhelming feeling Si knew the real story about what happened to Marcus.

The questions I need to focus on now are "why" and "how" he's involved.

As she left and got into her car, her thoughts momentarily turned to how she was feeling. *There have only been a couple of episodes of dizziness recently. I'm so grateful my body is tolerating the medication Dr. Densmore prescribed. The headaches haven't increased either. That's a relief.*

MOLLY
(Baby Claire)

Claire Christine Crandall was delivered by C-section on May 22, at eight o'clock in the morning as scheduled. Sadie and Sophie joined both sets of grandparents for the vigil at the hospital. They had grown close to Molly, and they were there to support her and show her they cared about her and the baby. Weighing in at 7 pounds and measuring 21 inches with a head of thick black hair, she was a strong, healthy little angel innocently unaware of the devastating events leading up to her birth. A confusing mix of sadness and joy brought tears to all of them. The experience was exhausting. Marcus' parents would have to leave in a day or two, but her parents were staying a couple more weeks to help her through this time. Having them there with her was a tremendous relief to her.

She was doing as well as could be expected. Friends came to the hospital with beautiful bouquets of flowers and kind, loving words, wrapping her and the baby in a protective cocoon of love. Her sorrow cut through the rampart, deeply penetrating every ounce of her being, allowing her little comfort. Acutely aware of her responsibilities as a single parent, she wanted to live for her little girl, but she struggled to fight off the despair brought on by feelings of anxiety and depression. In her mind, she played the tape over and over again. *How could life do this to us? What did Marcus do to deserve this? This was supposed to be the happiest time of our lives.* A twisted hand of fate intruded on their lives and played a cruel trick on her. She desperately wanted to be victorious in overcoming the destruction and loss, but the darkness pressed heavily on her heart.

After a couple of days, mother and daughter were discharged from the hospital. In the coming weeks, Sophie and Sadie continued to support her at home with their time and friendship. She was grateful to both of them. Molly hesitatingly started attending the weekly professional counseling sessions they arranged for her. "Don't you worry about a thing, dear," her mother coaxed. "We'll be fine here until you get back. You go on and do the work you need to do with your counselor." Then, after her parents left to return to their home, Sophie often spent evenings with them. Hours were spent listening with a loving heart as Molly described her life with Marcus. Her words painted pictures and captured emotions so vivid and real, Sophie came to feel as though she had actually known him. It was wonderful hearing about him, and Molly needed to talk about him. "He was an exceptional person, Sophie. He really was. I know I'm biased, but that was made clear to me the very first time I met him. Others saw it too...coworkers, his college professors, all saw something special in him. Until the day he died, no matter where we were or how many people we were with, he had the ability to make me feel like I was the only person in the room. We were soulmates. I feel so incomplete without him. I'm not sure I'm going to be able to go forward without him."

Remarkably, when Molly was in the depths of despair, Sophie was able to be strong for her. "You're not alone, Molly. God walks with you. He will never leave you, and he will equip you with all that you need." Other times, when their talks left Sophie feeling forlorn and downhearted, Molly was somehow able to lift her up. The devastating life event that so coldly brought them together continued to weave their lives together in warmth and genuine caring. They were strengthened one by the other. As time passed, the balm of friendship and the counseling sessions helped

Molly move forward toward the light with each new day.

All too soon, the weeks marched on. Sitting beside each other in the den as Claire slept between them, Molly and Sophie could hardly believe it was already mid-July. Little Claire was now a little over two months old. They hadn't spoken about the ongoing investigation recently, so Molly was moved to inquire about it. Not wanting to upset her by giving her too much information, Sophie guarded what she said. With conviction, she assured Molly they would find the person or persons responsible. Molly silently nodded and said, "I know you will. Your dedication to this case goes beyond that of a job, and I want you to know how much I appreciate how hard you're working for Claire and me. It means the world to me, and you give me hope. I'm worried about you, though. I can see in your face the toll it's taking on your health."

Sophie smiled and nodded as she took Molly's hand. "I'm pushing myself, but when I close the case and put it behind us, I promise to stow myself away at the cottage and rest. Thank you for your concern, my friend."

Soft smiles lit their faces as they looked at each other. Simultaneously, they turned their attention to Claire. Just then, her angelic little body began to twitch. Two tiny feet began a pedaling-like motion. With arms raised, she began to stretch her fragile little limbs and awaken with a yawn as soft as the flutter of butterfly wings.

CHIP AND BRIDGET
(Devastating News)

As the steamy hot month of July progressed, Sophie's health deteriorated. She was putting in long hours of investigative work on the Crandall case. On top of that, there was the stress of meeting column deadlines and trying to evoke avid interest and loyalty from the readers of her blog. All of this continued to wear Sophie down physically. The investigation required that she spend more time in Havendale, so she was writing from her home office and seeing more of Quinn, Sadie, and her parents, Chip and Bridget, during lunch breaks.

By now, they were all acutely aware of the toll the stress was taking

The Narrow Gate

on her. Each of them expressed their concern both to Sophie and to each other. Sadie was especially anxious because of the still present memory of the shadowy premonition-like scare she hadn't been able to identify back in the spring. Had she been mistaken when she decided the experience was a harbinger concerning Marcus and Molly? Was the premonition really about Sophie? She had doubts. In recent weeks, she questioned Sophie relentlessly about her health. Unbeknownst to all of them, Sophie's headaches and dizziness had been occurring with more frequency and intensity in spite of the medication. Her inner voice was urging her to make another appointment with Dr. Densmore. With the expectation of nothing more from him than perhaps stronger pills, she disregarded the warning and put it off. She convinced herself her time would be better spent on her column and the Crandall case.

Recent developments in the case put her in dogged pursuit to overturn the last piece of the puzzle, which would hand over the prize that named the culprit or culprits responsible for the financial maneuvering of the Hovland funds. She was now unshakable in the belief that embezzlement was what led to the death of Marcus. She was working closely with a consulting CPA firm. With their help, she felt sure all the financial pieces of the puzzle would fall into place soon. A craving for the opportunity to look Molly in the eye and tell her they got the evil-monger that killed Marcus filled her.

As focused as she was on the case, continual nagging thoughts made her feel she shouldn't, in good conscience, put off being honest with her family. She knew in her heart the time for telling them the awful news was at hand. Shortly after learning of her tumor, Sophie had sought ongoing counseling from Kier Jordahl, her pastor, in order to keep moving forward in her own acceptance and also for the help she would need to someday prepare her family.

Hours at night were spent searching her heart and praying for the wisdom

The Narrow Gate

to find the right words. The irony in that did not escape her. She was a gifted linguist, and as a professional writer she reaped a harvest of joy and fulfillment from her gift as well as many professional awards. Yet, she found herself barren, unsure and unable to produce the words and sentences she needed in this situation. She was filled with dread as she tried again and again to put herself in their place. In her mind, she conjured up a host of scenarios in hopes of preparing herself, in order to be better equipped to say the right things to comfort them. Sophie rehearsed words and thoughts in her mind, in the car, and aloud in the shower. Over and over in her mind, she rehearsed the words that would reveal her secret to them and shatter their worlds. She had so much love and respect for her parents. She didn't want to even imagine the effect her death would have on them.

It was late July, and the temperature was a balmy 90 degrees with a humidity reading of 96 percent. Sophie was alone in her home office, distracted by thoughts of needing to tell her parents about the tumor.

Mom and Dad are both seventy-four now. Dad has had a long career in town as the pharmacist at Monson's Drug Store. For forty years, he filled prescriptions and dispensed sage pharmacology knowledge to locals and area residents as well. Mom taught health at the Havendale Community College on an as-needed basis until she was well into her sixties. She's been a wonderful role model for me. She's in fabulous shape for a woman her age. They're both still physically active and in good health.

Sophie breathed deeply and sighed a long sigh. Her thoughts continued, *The local food shelf depends on them; they're devoted volunteers. They adore Sadie and me, and they love Ted just as if he were one of their own. They took such an active part in the lives of Seth, Sydney, and Christian when they were growing up. Dad was a basketball fanatic! How many years did he volunteer as the B-team coach? He's so proud of himself for never missing a practice session or a game for either of Sadie's boys.* In her mind, she pictured them in the stands at a game long ago. She heard Sadie's voice teasing, *"Mom, you applaud louder and holler more comments and words of encouragement from the stands than most of the other parents put together."*

Sydney was a gifted musician and dancer. *I can still see her on stage in her frilly little yellow tu-tu doing that bumble bee number. Oh, my gosh! I think she was about four years old. That was too cute! I know Mom and Dad sat through more recitals than they care to remember. They wouldn't have missed any of it.* She bowed her head as she let out a little laugh. *To this day, their house is filled with pictures of the kids. Every handmade gift the kids made for them is still proudly displayed in a special place of honor. They are exceptional parents. We are so blessed to have them in our lives.*

She was pushing herself to complete paperwork for her attorney and writing an article for her column.

Completing the legal forms hadn't been an easy task for her, but it felt good to be able to check it off her list of things to do for today. Completing the job was like releasing a 100-pound weight from her mind. Feelings of melancholy and loneliness plagued her a good part of the morning. Struggling to lift her spirits, she mentally comforted herself by recalling Philippians 4:6-7. She had committed the passage to memory years ago when worry and anxiety threatened to sabotage her career as a new investigative reporter. *"Don't worry about anything; instead pray about everything. Tell God what you need, and thank Him for all He has done. If you do this, you will experience God's peace, which is far more wonderful than the human mind can understand. His peace will guard your hearts and minds as you live in Christ Jesus."* Sophie stopped writing, dropped to her knees, and prayed a heartfelt prayer of praise and thanksgiving. *Remember, too, your thoughts create your emotions, Sophie Beth. Think about what is good in your life.*

Affirmations were an automatic part of her day by now. She breathed five deep breaths and chanted them. Slowly rising and feeling somewhat refreshed and inspired, she turned her thoughts back to finishing her column. *Just a few more lines before a final reread.* Within moments, she hit "save" and began silently reading:

What is it that makes you special to others? What do you want others to remember and perhaps, miss about you when you no longer walk this earth? Do you know what you want from each day you have left on this earth? If you knew when you would die, what things would you want to accomplish or complete before leaving this earth? Are there places you would want to go? Do you know how you would want to live out your life in your remaining days? These may be tough questions to answer for many of us. End-of-life is not something one usually gives much thought to while the minutes and hours of a day race by as we are busily going about our daily lives.

Many of you who read my column regularly have come to know that I long ago adopted and applied the Boy Scout philosophy of "always be prepared" to my own life. Being prepared can help ensure that we act in ways that carry out our values and beliefs on a daily basis. Put into action, these values and beliefs develop our character. They are the measure of worth and importance we give ourselves and our lives. Sometimes, they are the measure of respect and value we give to others as well...definitely something worth thinking about.

Currently, I am investigating the death of Marcus Crandall, a young CPA with the firm of Hyshum and Lester, Havendale, WI. I didn't know Marcus when he walked this earth, but since his death last May, I have grown to know him through his devoted wife, Molly. In the weeks and months since his death, Molly and I have spent hours together talking about the man and husband he was. Marcus lived his life one day at a time, focusing his thoughts and his heart on what really mattered to him. He was a loving and faithful husband who dedicated himself to his wife, friends, and family. Marcus' mornings started with a heartfelt affirmation to his lovely wife of what she meant to him. "He was a guy," Molly confessed to me. "It wasn't always said the way Prince Charming would say it, but it was real and it meant the world to me. It was the highlight of my day."

I can tell you that it was not only Molly who suffered a great loss at the premature death of this fine young man, but the community of Havendale and his precious infant daughter, Claire, as well. He never got the chance to demonstrate what kind of father he would have been because his daughter was born just weeks after his untimely death. Fate stepped in and robbed him of that precious gift.

But we can get an idea of what might have been through the words of his friends: I spoke to Brad Crookston, a childhood friend from Maine who was obviously struggling with the tragic loss when we spoke, "We grew up together, and he was my best friend for over thirty years. Loyal and dependable...I could count on him when I needed help even when we were apart geographically. I can't think of a time when he ever let me down." Golf partner and fellow bicyclist, Glen Diamond, described his friend: "True to his word. I could set my clock by his dependability. If he told you he was going to do something for you, he did it. It wasn't just idle talk. He was just an incredibly wonderful friend." Director of Havendale's West Side Boys Home, Fred Winthrop, praised him for his volunteer service saying, "His tireless efforts and influential guiding hand will be sorely missed. He had such a gift for combining patience and compassion with just the right amount of tough love. That was a highly effective combination for the boys he sponsored, and he achieved significant success in changing their lives. He was just so decent to the boys. I guess that's because he really cared about them. We're all going to miss him."

Marcus Crandall had everything to live for, but swiftly and mysteriously, his life ended on a beautiful spring day. Was he prepared to die? Had he lived each day in a manner that would have brought him assurance he had made the most of the days he was given? Had he thought about what made him special to others? These questions will have to go unanswered.

He has been described by those who shared his life as a man of deep character and compassion, exemplifying a life well lived. It mattered that Marcus Crandall lived. He will not soon be forgotten.

With a few more strokes on the keyboard, the article was submitted to the *Daily*, just barely meeting her deadline. Slowly, she leaned back in her chair. A heavy sigh escaped, ushering out the feelings of sadness that filled her. Softly she uttered, "Lord, thank you for the gift of Marcus. Thank you for the wonderful man he was. Thank you for the example he gave us. Thank you for the blessing he was to those around him. Help us remember him and the life he lived and the lessons he taught us. Bless Claire with the blessing of always having caring, loving adults in her life to guide her and keep her safe. I ask this, Lord, in the name of Jesus. Amen."

The time had come. A driving force overtook her. She was moved to take action and call Sadie and her parents. She just suddenly felt it. It was time to tell them about her tumor, and she had faith God would bring the words to her. Thoughts of Sydney and her upcoming wedding were eating away at her, filling her with absolute dread. As it so happened, the call to her mother revealed Sadie and Quinn were there with her. "Your dad went down to Ralph's to pay his bill, but he'll be back soon. Come on over, honey. We'd all love to see you."

The furnace-like heat in the garage wrapped itself around her as she entered the car.

Sophie pulled into the driveway and parked behind Sadie's car, pausing to really focus on the four-story white clapboard house in front of her. The structure had been a home to her and her family for so many years. She loved the open wrap porch with its multicolored porch poles and inviting swing. She smiled as she got out of the car. *The love inside this house kept me warm and protected me throughout the storms of life just as this building provided shelter from the seasonal storms of summers and winters past.* It suddenly dawned on her: *Telling my family about my illness will most likely turn out to be like wrapping myself in a warm blanket on a cold, stormy day.* She hadn't consciously thought about what their support would mean to her.

Suddenly, the feelings of weakness and vulnerability she felt gave way to despicable thoughts of selfishness and the self-indulgence she began to see in herself. In the stifling heat and her confusion, she questioned her motives for being there. *Is this for me or for them? Am I really just being needy? Is it best for them to know? Oh, I don't know. I don't know what to do.* She thought about fleeing, but she noticed the front door was open. She was quickly greeted with a sloppy, wet kiss from Blondie, her mother's caramel-colored Cocker Spaniel. Her mother stood in the doorway motioning for her to come in. Thankfully, a tall glass of strawberry lemonade and the cool inside air helped restore her emotional equilibrium as she sat amid Quinn and her family members. *I'm not alone. God will grant me the words. He will give me the strength and courage I need to do this. He will equip me with all that I need to tell them and to comfort them.*

Her father arrived home. "Sophie, it's good to see you, honey. Are you

The Narrow Gate

getting enough sleep? You look tired, Soph."

"That's why I'm here, Dad. Come, let's all go into the den and sit down. There is something I need to tell you."

The five of them settled in, and Sophie began. "We don't usually begin our visits with prayer, but this isn't going to be like our usual visits, so would you please pray with me?"

All four pairs of eyes lifted and were squarely riveted on Sophie. Sadie and Quinn arose from the couch simultaneously and walked over to her chair. Squatting down, they each found a place on the floor to sit aside Sophie. Sadie reached for her hand as Quinn began to gently stroke her arm in a show of love and support. Bridget moved to the edge of her chair in nervous anticipation of what Sophie had to say. Just opposite her, in his favorite chair, Chip sat quietly and motionless. Each of them trembled inside. Each of them knew, without knowing, the words Sophie was about to speak would not only be devastating, but quite possibly life-threatening for her.

"Heavenly Father, you are so good. You brought me into this wonderful family and blessed the five of us with enduring love for one another. You provided this wonderful home where we cared for one another and grew stronger as a family as we experienced all that life brought to our lives. You continually care for us and watch over us, giving us all that we need. Your love protects us from the storms in each season of our lives just as this house has sheltered us from the rain of thunderstorms and the cold of raging snow storms in the dead of winter. We love you, Lord; and, we thank you and praise you for your faithfulness. Our hope lies in you as we face the current storm brewing in my life. Grant us your peace, Lord. Grant us your comfort and assurance that you are with us. Help us to know the warmth of your love. We ask this in the loving name of Jesus. Amen."

"It's ok, Sophie. You can tell us. We'll help you." Sadie whispered.

The Narrow Gate

Quinn's stomach was tied in knots. She could barely speak the words, "We love you, Soph."

Sophie looked into their eyes. Her heart was full, brimming with love for them. Out of that love, she found her voice. Quietly and tenderly she began to reveal her secret as she found herself saying the words, "I have a brain tumor. Dr. Densmore diagnosed it in May," she nodded affirming. "I went to see him because I was having headaches and dizziness. He said it's inoperable. He thought I probably had six months."

The quiet in the room was deafening. Only the ticking of the old Seth Thomas clock, standing atop the oak shelf, was heard as the pendulum swayed from side to side. Each of them was too stunned to speak.

Bridget moved to the edge of her chair in nervous anticipation of what Sophie had to say.

Chip's heart broke. His body physically ached for his little girl. She was a grown woman with renowned talent, but she was still his little girl.

Chip And Bridget

The color drained from his face. His head hung as he sat dazed, feeling utterly helpless.

Coming out of Sadie's embrace, Sophie opened her eyes and noticed her father. Urgently, she broke free and raced to his side. Crouching down and gently placing her hand under his chin, she raised his head. Lovingly, she looked into his eyes. With a soft, soothing voice, she spoke words of comfort, "I'm okay with this, Dad. You know I love the Lord. We're all going home to be with Him someday. My day is on the calendar, that's all." She gently wrapped her arms around him and held him close as his tears spilled over, washing his cheeks in a caustic solution of pain, sadness, and grief.

The other three quietly left the room to allow them time alone together. They followed each other into the kitchen. Bridget began to busy herself making coffee, knowing they would be together in conversation and support the rest of the day. Sadie frantically began thinking and talking about plans to seek lifesaving treatment for Sophie. Quinn agreed there had to be something that could be done to save her.

CHIP

(A Father's Love)

Days later, Sophie found herself hip-deep in cardboard boxes filled with clothing and other items to be given away. It was an uneventful Saturday. She had the day to herself. Because of the dizzy spells, she was staying in town for the weekend rather than taking a chance of driving the distance to the cabin. Her energy level was running low, but she pushed herself all morning to clean out her bedroom closet and drawers. Each box was labeled with the name of a worthy charity. It was 11:30. As she glanced at her list of things to do, she finished her last bite of lunch. Settling her bill with Ralph and Stella was

The Narrow Gate

listed as her next chore. She briefly entertained the idea of waiting and going later in the day when it would be cooler. Quickly, she dismissed those thoughts, telling herself: *Stella will expect me to come for coffee. I don't really want to miss that time with her either.* As she carried her lunch plate to the sink, the doorbell rang. Slowly, she set down the dish and began to make her way to the front room. Rounding the corner from the kitchen heading into the parlor, she could see the outline of a man. He was standing with his back to her as she looked through the etched, beveled glass in the ornate door. Instantly, she recognized the man as her father. He turned and faced her as she opened the door. Seeing his grave face made her gasp. He looked drawn and very, very old to Sophie. "Oh! Dad! Oh, Dad, come in. Come in and sit down." Feelings of fear for his well-being began to seep through her whole body. "Are you all right?"

He responded by slowly stepping into the parlor. "Here, sit here on the couch." She directed. "I'm going to get you a glass of cold water."

When she returned and handed him the glass, she settled on the couch close beside him. As she looked into his eyes, the familiar look of grief met her gaze. She had seen that look a million times on the faces of the families and survivors of crime victims. Seeing the devastation on her father's face cut her to the core. She struggled with her thoughts. *What do I say to him? Oh, my gosh, what have I done to him? I shouldn't have told him. He looks so fragile!*

"I had to see you, Sophie," he said softly with a voice filled with anguish. "I had to come and see my girl. I haven't been able to sleep. I haven't been able to think of anything else but you since you told us about the tumor. I've been doing a lot of thinking these past few days, Soph. The thought of losing you has been unbearable. There are things I want, no, things I need to say to you, honey." He gently reached for her hand and cupped it tenderly between both of his hands.

"I'm not as good with words as you are, dear, but I'm going to do my best to try to make you understand. You know I've never been one to share my feelings much. I guess I was wrong about that, but I hope you don't hold it against me. I just never felt comfortable saying words like that out loud."

Sophie nodded her head. "No, Dad, no. There is nothing for you to regret. You have been a wonderful father to me. I could never have asked for a better father." The lump in her throat grew bigger with each word she struggled to utter.

"When you were born," he continued, "I guess I was young and egotistical, because I was disappointed when the doctor came out to the waiting room and told me I had a daughter. You see, I had my heart set on having a son. In those days, we didn't have those tests the young parents have today. We didn't know if we were having a boy or a girl. Your mother said she didn't care what we got just as long as you were whole and healthy. I wanted a boy to carry on my name. Oh, I had plans for the things we would do together. There was no doubt in my mind that my son would grow up to really be somebody."

He went on to say, "I can remember the day you were born, honey, just as if it were yesterday. It didn't take more than a second for me to fall head-over-heels in love with you the first time I looked at you. I was just so pleased. I got over the notion of being disappointed quickly enough. The point is, honey, you have never disappointed me. You have been my greatest joy. I love you, and I am so proud of you. I'm proud of all that you have accomplished in your career, but I am most proud of you for the person that you are. You were beautiful when I first laid eyes on you, and you still are."

With an adoring look, "You're a beautiful woman, honey, but you're a magnificent woman because of the person you are on the inside. I love the ways you show others how much you care about them. I love the kindness that I see you show to all of us.

I love your patience and gentleness with Sadie's kids. You were always there for them. I love the way you live your life in service to God. I love the way you always give 110 percent to solving the crimes you investigate in order to give the families the answers they need. I love that you never give up on a case, and you never take the responsibility lightly. You're one of the bravest people I know, Soph. I love your intelligence, your strength, and your honesty. I love you for the honor and respect you always show to your mother and me. Oh, honey, I could go on and on."

He looked at her with a resigned smile on his face. He was unsure of himself, but it was too important to him not to get this right, so he continued. "As I said, I'm not good with the words." He bowed his head and continued, "I just need to make sure that you know I am so honored to be your father." Raising his head and looking at Sophie, he struggled to say, "You have been more than any father could ever hope for. You're a constant source of pride to me. I will love you forever, honey. It just kills me that I can't fix this for you because I can't bear to lose you." He was unable to say anything more.

Sophie leaned forward and embraced him. With a heavy heart she reassuringly whispered, "Thank you, Dad. I love you with all my heart. You have been the perfect father to me." They held each other close while they both cried silent tears. After a while, they got up and moved outside to sit on the patio. Nothing more needed to be said. They sat there in solitude, understanding each other, appreciating each other, and loving each other.

STELLA

(Heart-To-Heart)

The two o'clock sun was sitting high in the late July sky, promising punishing heat. Immediately, the relentless intensity of the heat wrapped itself around her like cellophane on a bowl of leftovers as Sophie crawled into her car. She encountered a light flow of traffic as she cautiously steered her car along the winding road. The Tiger Lilies were blooming early this year. Just ahead, she delighted in the sight of a lush roadside border of bright orange and intense yellow petals symmetrically arched, basking in the heat of the brilliant summer sun.

Arriving at her destination, she sat parked off to the side of the old gas station for a little while with the engine turned off. A deep sigh escaped. The headaches, often pounding, were occurring more frequently. The bouts of dizziness sometimes brought her to her knees. Today had been a tough day so far. She felt vulnerable and heavily burdened after the time spent with her father earlier. Fearing she might break down with Stella, she hesitated to get out of the car. She considered coming back another time; however, as she lifted her head and looked out the window, she saw Ralph noticing her. Stella also stood at the window eagerly looking out in her direction.

I can't do this alone, Lord. Be near me I pray, and give me strength. Stoically, she reached to open the car door. Within seconds, she found herself warmly greeted by Ralph and then passed off to Stella's warm embrace.

"Ah, honey, I'm so glad to see ya. I know'd you'd be coming, soon. I've been looking forward to seeing ya. The coffee is fresh. Now, girl, you just sit yerself down over here in your chair where it's nice and cool while I pour us a cup. We'll have us a nice visit. Scoot, Mr. Dievers. Go on. Now that seat is for our guest. Your place is over there, you know that. Now, you go over there. Go on."

Sophie secretly chuckled as she slid a check to cover her bill across the table to where Stella would sit. Mr. Dievers was king of the castle, such as it was. He was very seldom rebuked. It looked to her that he was momentarily thinking of staging a protest, but he jumped down off the chair and waddled off into the next room.

It was a slow time in the day. They chatted unbothered by Ralph or customers coming in and out for about half an hour. Out of nowhere, Stella beseeched Sophie, "What's troublin' ya, my darlin' girl? I can see it in your eyes, and I hear it in your voice. Come, now, unburden your heart. Maybe I can help."

The flood gates opened. Sophie crumbled into a million pieces as she cried out, "No, Stella, you can't help. No one can help me."

Grasping for Sophie's hands, Stella responded, "Gracious, you precious child, whatever has got you so distressed? Come, now; you tell Stella. You let it all out."

They moved from the front area of the station into the cozy living quarters in the back. Minutes turned into hours. Ensconced, as her dear friend poured out her heart along with the dire details of her tumor, Stella's heart crumbled.

The conversation deepened. Like a ping-pong ball swatted back and forth over the net, Sophie took her turn talking as Stella listened, and Stella took her turn as Sophie listened. Their faith never wavered, but the flesh faltered, and they drew strength and renewal from each other as they cried. It took Sophie's breath away to learn Stella, too, made the same life-living decisions two years ago when the diagnosis of lung cancer fell upon her. The way Stella and Ralph lived their daily lives joyously serving

The Narrow Gate

others made more sense to her now. She was touched to hear what her visits had meant to Stella. Thinking it was she who was inspired by Stella and Ralph, she had no idea Stella drew the same gift from her in their times spent together.

"You give me a precious gift, girlie. You give me the gift of yerself."

Daylight eventually gave way to dusk, and still they talked. Finally, Sophie stood, preparing to leave. Stella's parting words were, "Remember, God's gracious favor is all we need, Sophie, girl. His power works best in our weakness, and you and I are desperate for Him. We're in good hands." Profound love and gratitude filled each of their hearts, and they expressed that love to each other as they embraced before Sophie left and walked toward her car.

She began reflecting on the effects the unburdening of her illness to her family and friends was having. The heat inside the car was stifling, so she turned on the engine and ran the air conditioner. The cool air was slow in coming and provided little relief. She paused for a moment as she sat solemnly behind the wheel, her head hanging low. Filled with regret, she brought up the mental picture of the look on her father's face when she told him of her tumor. *The news hit him with the force of a knock-out punch. He's taking it so hard, and it's taking a huge toll on him.* Her thoughts moved on to Sadie who had recounted for all of them the premonition she had last spring. Sophie winced as she brought to mind the tearful voice of her sister: *"I blame myself for not seeing what the truth is now revealing as the writing on the wall."*

Sophie remembered, *The next day, Sadie sprang into action like a mother bear protecting her cub. Using all of her contacts at the Havendale Hospital, she bypassed Dr. Densmore and set up an appointment at the Mayo Clinic for a second opinion. She was determined there was a medical procedure that could be done.* Sophie opined, *I do believe Sadie would be willing to die herself trying to save me.*

The thought brought a loving smile to Sophie's face. *The earliest appointment she was able to get was in August. Do I dare to hope the doctors will have good news for me?*

Suddenly, she felt very tired. She shifted into drive and pulled onto Main Street. Overcome with exhaustion, she went straight to bed when she got home. Rhubarb cuddled close. Sweet sleep soon enveloped the two of them, carrying them through the night.

DR. KENDALL DENSMORE

(What's Going On?)

In his early forties and still full of ambition, dashing Kendall Densmore arrived in Havendale on a beautiful August morning. The dog days of summer ushered in cooler morning temperatures, a welcome relief from the stifling humidity of the past two weeks. The air was still. Birds chattered in the treetops.

Becoming part of his father's practice wasn't on his radar screen. However, unseen events, soon to fall into place, would result in just that. After several months of pesky phone calls, he had given in to his mother's insistent urgings that he come and check on his father's health.

The Narrow Gate

It was Friday. His plan was to spend the next three days with his parents, and then return to his practice as a highly respected radiologist in San Diego. His flight into Minneapolis was uneventful—just the way he liked it. Staff at the rental car agency had been effectively efficient and Minnesota-nice.

He had left Havendale at eighteen to attend college out east. Afterwards, he went right on to Northeastern University School of Medicine. Other than a rare holiday visit here and there, he hadn't been back in fifteen years. He now saw himself as a Californian, and driving into Havendale on Highway 10 from the south he admitted to himself he was not glad to be back. As he drove through Main Street, the changes he noticed were dramatic. Since his last visit, it seemed to him Havendale had transposed itself from a rural, blue collar horse-town to a chic tourist attraction. He felt indifferent to the change, but he noticed it.

Before long, he was unpacking his bags in his old bedroom with his mother in tears. Twisting her handkerchief as she sat on his bed, she lamented, "I'm afraid, Kendall. Your father shouldn't be practicing. He should have retired last spring. I've tried talking to him, but he never wants to talk about it. What if he has misdiagnosed some of his patients? There could be untold consequences for them and the law suits could be staggering."

"Mother, I'm sure you're overreacting. It can't be as bad as all that. Nurse Addie and his colleagues would have said something."

"They have," she countered. "I've tried to tell you, but you kept insisting I was overreacting, just as you are now. His symptoms come and go. It's not always noticeable, and I think he's good at covering things up, too," she continued.

"All right, I'm here now, and I'll be on my way to his office just as soon as I finish hanging up a few more things."

She had had enough of his dismissive attitude. She aggressively reached out for the trousers in his hand, and shooed him away. "Go now," she said tersely. "I'll finish up here."

The house was a short distance from the office. Backing out of the driveway, he wondered if any of the old neighborhood kids still remained in town. He hadn't seen or heard from any of them in decades. He wasn't really interested in seeing any of them while he was in town. He just wondered.

As he opened the door and entered his father's once thriving office, he was struck by the morgue-like atmosphere. There were no patients in the waiting room. No one was sitting behind the admitting desk. He found his father, looking considerably older than the last time he saw him, fast asleep on a table in one of the examining rooms. Nurse Addie was visibly embarrassed when she realized what he had seen.

"What's going on here?" he demanded. She motioned for him to follow her to another room where she closed the door and pulled out chairs for each of them to sit.

Addie had been Dr. Densmore's nurse for almost forty years, so she had known Kendall as a young boy. She couldn't help noticing how distinguished and professional he appeared. "Kendall, it's wonderful to see you again."

His body language made it obvious to her that he was neither happy about what he had just seen, nor was he in the mood for exchanging niceties with her. She hastily proceeded to explain.

"Your father is having a bad day, Kendall. I encouraged him to lie down and rest. His health has been deteriorating the past few months. I've been keeping a very close eye on him here at the office. The changes were subtle at first. I noticed little things like some forgetfulness and at times he was disoriented. When I realized things were progressing, I stopped accepting new patients. I've limited his contact with patients to minor care on his good days with my direct supervision. His colleagues have been filling in for him."

"I spoke to your mother about it. She has tried to talk to him. He refuses to listen to her. She's at her wit's end in knowing what to do. She needs you, and I'm so glad you're here. The deterioration has been more rapid just recently. He's at a point where he can't be allowed to practice medicine at all anymore, Kendall. You've got to take him home. Make him realize he needs medical attention. I suspect Alzheimer's disease, but he has not been diagnosed. Doctors don't make good patients, you know."

It was somewhat humbling for Kendall to learn he had been wrong to brush off his mother's pleas for help. However, he was more shaken after seeing his father firsthand, by the realization his lifelong medical career had come to an abrupt end. He had always seen his father as a strong, decisive man devoted to the care of his patients and the practice of medicine.

He was solemn on their short drive home, saddened by his father's confused state. He also felt a sense of urgency to return to the office to look at medical files. He was trying not to panic in light of the situation.

When he returned, Addie was able to assure him there was only one patient that required further attention. "I just pulled the file up yesterday, and I find it miraculous you're here just at this time to offer a second opinion. I think that must be a sign of some kind. I'm going to take it as that. That's the reason I'm making an exception by showing you the medical records even though you are not her doctor."

Addie opened a file on the screen and said, "I think it may be a perfect fit with your area of expertise. The patient's name is Sophie Stangler. Her father is a good friend of your father, so you may remember the family. She was originally diagnosed in early May when I was out sick. I suffer from seasonal allergies, and I was having quite a time with the high pollen count last spring. When I returned to work, there was no indication to suggest I needed to follow up on her. In fact, Dr. Densmore never mentioned her to me.

The diagnosis was a brain tumor. I've seen enough of those scans to know this one is different. I'm guessing, but it looks more like an aneurysm to me. If I'm right, you're just the one to diagnose it."

Kendall frowned as he leaned in to get a closer look. He briefly studied the various screens before glancing back at Addie with a look that showed newfound respect. "Get her in here today if possible."

SOPHIE

(The Missing Puzzle Piece)

"Hallelujah!" Sophie shouted to the consultants who had just offered up enough evidence to put Danny Lockwood away for embezzling $500,000.00 dollars. "I feel certain that's what led to the murder of Marcus Crandall," she crowed.

The theft was extensive, going well beyond the Hovland account. "For some time now, we've been pretty sure about how the murder was perpetrated. Detective Sims and I have had our suspicions all along about who was involved. Without this evidence to prove motive, our hands have been tied. This is thrilling news. Thank you."

The Narrow Gate

Park and Sophie both stood up and shook hands with the consultants. As soon as they left the room, Sophie impulsively turned to Park and threw her arms around his neck while laying her head back shouting, "Yes, yes, yes!" The exuberant smile covering her face quickly turned to a look of stunned disbelief as she lowered her head and met his staring gaze front and center. She immediately realized what she had done, and began pulling away in total embarrassment. "Oh, I'm sorry, Park. I didn't mean anything by it."

A deep chuckle escaped his lips before he grabbed her and lifted her up off her feet swinging her around in circles. The two of them were giddy with excitement, but the merriment ceased when Sophie grew dizzy. Park slowly lowered her feet to the floor as he continued to hold on to her for support. He gently lowered her onto a nearby chair. She closed her eyes, desperately wishing for it to go away. "Lean back while I go and get you some water." He moved swiftly, and returned within seconds.

Sophie

"Oh, I guess that was too much excitement for an old gal like me," she offered sheepishly.

"Nonsense! That dizziness didn't come from excitement." He admonished. "What's going on Sophie? You've looked like death-warmed-over for the past month. Why won't you tell me what's wrong so I can help you?"

"Why, you sweet talker, you," she said softly. "Pretty words like that are likely to make a girl's head spin," she joked. "I've just been working too hard. You're a slave driver. You know that, don't you?"

Park was having none of it. "You're hiding something from me, Sophie, and I'm taking you to the clinic right now."

With that, he picked her up, carried her out the door, and deposited her in the squad car.

"Oh, stop, Park. This isn't necessary. I appreciate your concern. The dizziness will clear up. Just give me a few more minutes."

Park was in full take-charge mode as he responded, "Buckle your seat belt, Stangler. We're going for a ride whether you like it or not."

Her continued pleas and protests went ignored. The dizziness didn't let up as they drove to the clinic. Within minutes, he was carrying her into the clinic. Nurse Addie could hardly believe her eyes when she saw Sophie come through the door. She had just barely left the voice message on her office phone requesting Sophie return for a visit as soon as possible.

DR. KENDALL DENSMORE

(Tears Of Joy)

"Dr. Kendall!" Nurse Addie urgently summoned.

Dr. Kendall hastily met the three of them in the waiting room. He briefly explained, "My father isn't well. I'm afraid it could be dementia or Alzheimer's. He won't be practicing medicine anymore. I've driven him home, and he's resting comfortably. Nurse Addie and I have reviewed your scans, Sophie. I'd like you to come with me to his office so we can talk. I have good news for you." Confused, Park and Sophie followed both he and Addie to his father's office.

The dizziness finally passed as they sat in rapt attention, listening

The Narrow Gate

to what Dr. Kendall was telling them. Park and Sophie clung to each other, crying tears of joy and relief in response to the incredible news that Sophie's brain tumor was a misdiagnosed aneurysm. As a radiologist, he assured her it was treatable. They listened, with hearts soaring, as he triumphantly described the four hour "coiling" procedure.

"A catheter carrying coils and platinum is threaded inside the aneurysm, essentially blocking blood flow to the characteristic bulge. It's a lifesaving procedure that will prevent the aneurysm from exploding. It will also get rid of your headaches and the dizziness as well."

Sophie wanted him to do the procedure, and steps were put in place to have it done in San Diego as soon as possible.

She was troubled by the news of Kendall's father. "I want you to know I love your father, Kendall. I'm so sorry he's ill. He's been a wonderful friend and doctor to our family for many years. We've treasured him, and this misdiagnosis won't change how we feel about him. If there's anything my family and I can do to help you and your mother, please don't hesitate to call on us."

He was very grateful and expressed his appreciation for her father's friendship to his father over the years and for her understanding and loyalty to his father. He was concerned for both of his parents. He promised to contact Sophie and her father as soon as he had a medical diagnosis for his father.

As she and Park left the clinic and walked outside, her feelings were indescribable. Feelings of deep sadness for her beloved doctor ricocheted off feelings of intense joy from knowing she was going to live. She felt incredibly blessed to have Park by her side. Secretly, she acknowledged the feelings she felt for him stirring within her heart.

His heart, too, was burning with feelings for her.

"What now?" he asked hesitantly.

Instinctively, she answered, "Make the call to have Danny brought in. I want to know if he and that self-indulgent, money-hungry Si killed Marcus or if they hired someone else to do it. Call me just as soon as you're done interrogating them. Right now, I'm going to call my family. I want to tell them the good news in person."

"No, I meant what now for us," he clarified softly.

Sophie didn't hesitate to look him square in the eye as she responded boldly, "I have feelings for you, Park. I realize now I've been denying those feelings. I thought I would be dead in just a few more months. Miraculously, I've been given a second chance to live. I can't wait to start living it with you, if you'll have me."

Park leaned in, initiating the kiss that sealed the bargain between them, answering her with more feeling and commitment than any words of acceptance he could have uttered. They looked into each other's eyes, smiled, and simultaneously reached for their cell phones. They would talk to each other later.

Sadie picked up on the second ring. Sophie began barking orders. "Sadie, call Quinn and Molly and tell them to get over to Mom and Dad's, a.s.a.p. I'll pick up Stella and meet you there. I'll explain when I get there."

Without hesitation or questioning what was going on, Sadie complied. "Right away." Sophie was ecstatic. She dialed Kier's number and silently prayed as she waited for him to pick up the phone. *Lord, thank you for your gracious favor. I am so grateful to know that I have more time here on this earth with those I love. I praise you and thank you. Amen."*

"Hello. Pastor Kier speaking. How can I help you?"

"Kier, it's me, Sophie. Can you get over to Mom and Dad's a.s.a.p.? Everything's ok. I just want you to be there for the news I have to share."

"I'm on my way, Sophie."

Sophie started the car and headed for the gas station to pick up Stella. Her emotions raced higher and higher. *I'm going to live. I'm going to live.*

DANNY

(The Wrong Choice)

Things were bustling at the Havendale Police Station the next day. Park had been there most of the night. He had been questioning Danny Lockwood, trying to break him down so he would cough up the details behind the murder of Marcus. Since his arrest, he continued to maintain his innocence.

Sophie came in around dawn feeling energized by her new prognosis. Since hearing from Park that Danny continued to deny any involvement, she was filled with an unshakable will to tear his story apart like a pit bull shredding newspaper. She knew he was the weaker of the two, and she suspected he had been a pawn in a scheme instigated by Si. She exchanged brief small talk with him as she sat down across the table from him. As she turned her recorder on, she looked him square in the eyes. With iron-willed determination to get him to talk, she proceeded. "You're going down even though I think Si was the instigator. I think you were just a pawn in his scheme, weren't you, Danny? I can't see you doing this on your own. Why did you go along with him, Danny? What did he have over you?"

The timing was right. He was worn down from lack of sleep. The stress of the continuous interrogations throughout the night made him more vulnerable. Finally, he reached his breaking point.

Like a geyser, the story poured forth from his lips. "I dallied with Si's wife. When Si discovered what was going on, he threatened to tell my wife. I begged him not to tell her. This wasn't the first time I had been unfaithful to her. She told me she would destroy

The Narrow Gate

me financially if I ever did it again. That was the leverage Si needed to force me to embezzle the funds which he was so desperate for in order to dig himself out of the financial pit he was in." Shaking his head, he recounted how Si wasn't concerned about his wife's indiscretion with him. His only concern was the money. With disgust, Danny continued. "He was almost salivating at the chance to get his hands on a large sum of money. I didn't have a choice. If my wife found out, I would have been ruined financially. I didn't have a choice."

Sophie didn't waiver in her pursuit to get all the answers from him she could. "Tell me what happened to Marcus, Danny."

At that point, he started to cry. In a small voice, through the sobs, the sighs, and the delayed remorse, he confessed, "Si pushed Marcus over the railing. That wasn't part of the plan. No one was supposed to get hurt. Si panicked. He told me he talked to Marcus just before he went out to the balcony. Marcus made a comment about trouble with one of his accounts. Si assumed he was on to me. After he pushed him, he ran to my office and told me what he'd done. He warned me if I said anything to anyone, he would tell the police Marcus had discovered I was embezzling, so I killed him. He had me. It's not my fault. I didn't have a choice." Spent and exhausted, Danny laid his arms and head on the table and sobbed.

"You had a choice, Danny," she admonished. "There's always a choice. You just made the wrong one." The heaviness of the sorrow she felt for Marcus, Molly, and Claire lay with the weight of a boulder on Sophie's heart as she got up and left the room.

PASTOR KIER

(Support For Stella)

Sophie had her surgery. It was now late August, and she was fully recovered. Her energy and stamina were back in full measure. She was back at work, as well as keeping up a full schedule with friends, family and community work.

The dwindling heat of summer loosened its grip. The night air was cool and refreshing. A host of stars twinkled in the clear night sky. Inside the church, the last session of Kier's class, "Living With Evil", was ending. It had been a six-week course offering healing and support to emergency personnel dealing with the everyday atrocities they faced on the job.

Participants were local law enforcement officers, social workers, EMTs, hospital personnel, and Sophie.

Kier Jordahl stood at the front of the small meeting room. "Great session, kids. Thanks for sharing your personal feelings about so many tough experiences. We've had some powerful sessions."

At thirty-one, Kier was the senior pastor at Sophie's church. He was a dynamic young man with a larger-than-life personality. Most of the attendees and Sophie were old enough to be his parents, but he enjoyed calling them "kids." Sophie often chuckled to herself when he did that because it reminded her of a time when she and Sadie were young girls living at home with their parents. She couldn't recall their ages, but she knew it was during their elementary school days. Distinctly, Sophie could hear Sadie's elfin-like voice in her memory now calling her *"Miss Happy Pants"* when she was in a sour mood. It always made her cry. She could see herself as a little girl running off, seeking motherly comfort and counsel to make Sadie stop. Kier meant it as a term of endearment, and everyone took it with good humor.

Sophie stood, and it felt good to stretch her legs after sitting for the past two hours. "Kier," she called out. "If you have a few minutes, I'd like to run an idea past you." He nodded to her in the affirmative, and motioned for her to follow him as he headed out the door. They walked together toward his office.

She recognized special gifts in him the first time she heard him speak, and over the years she had quickly volunteered more of her time at church in order to work with him on committees and special projects. In a short time, he became her spiritual mentor and they met regularly. The sessions took on new meaning and urgency to both of them after her brain tumor was diagnosed. Faithfully and compassionately, he guided her through her toughest, darkest times in some of their weekly sessions. Through his ongoing counsel, her strength was renewed. Serenely, she was able to continue walking the road of faith. When her aneurysm was diagnosed, they had rejoiced together at her deliverance. She felt tremendous gratitude for his guidance.

Concern for her friend, Stella, was sitting heavy on Sophie's heart, prompting her to take the action she was now taking. In the hour that followed, they lovingly laid the framework for a new class to offer support for those living with a terminal illness. They would call it "Sentenced to Live". Sophie would make sure Stella was a vital part of the class. "She has so much to offer the other participants, Kier. She's a very giving, loving person. Her service to God is offered up in a very unpretentious way. Yet, there is no denying the impact and effectiveness she has on the people she encounters day-to-day at that unassuming little gas station. I can attest to that personally. We never know do we, who God will place in our lives to be a blessing to us?"

SOPHIE

(God's Gracious Favor)

Indian summer ushered in a glorious September morning for the wedding. The temperature was a perfect 78 degrees. A vibrant sun shone down on the calm waters of Swan Lake. The garden was ablaze in a rainbow of colors, and a sweet aroma filled the air. Classical music played softly in the background.

Sophie's smile was radiant as she and her father stood arm-in-arm near a hedge of rose bushes. She was the picture of elegance dressed in a full length, fitted, off-the-shoulder, white gown. Her shoulder-length auburn hair was swept up atop her head. Cascading soft curls framed her face.

Sophie

She carried a fragrant bouquet of mixed flowers from her garden. As she looked around to all that was before her, she was once again in awe of the miraculous events that had taken place in her life, bringing her to this day.

The people she loved were seated on the front lawn on white cloth-covered chairs in silent anticipation under a scallop-edged canopy tent. Her dark blue eyes rested on beautiful Quinn, her loyal, lifelong friend, then moved on to her precious sister, Sadie and her husband, Ted. She was filled with love for each of them. She smiled as she caught the eyes of Ralph and Stella. As they had once long ago, the three of them managed to convince Eugene to take care of the station for the day so they could be here. *This day wouldn't have been the same without them,* she thought.

She continued to scan the crowd. The sight of Claire sleeping peacefully in her mother's arms with Molly's parents sitting on either side of her almost took her breath away. She

The Narrow Gate

could barely look away, but Seth, Sydney, Michael, and Christian caught her attention as they sat grinning and waving at her. Thoughts of standing next to Sydney at her wedding in December filled her with joy. Her dear mother, looking peaceful and happy, sat smiling in the front row. Lucie caught Sophie's eye. She also noticed neighbors from around the lake and coworkers from the *Daily* and the police department.

Finally, her eyes came to rest on the Densmores. Her heart was brimming with thanksgiving to see Jack with his wife and Kendall. The diagnosis had been Alzheimer's Disease. It was progressing. His presence meant he was having a good day; he would be able to recognize them.

She felt complete as she whispered softly, "Lord, I don't know when you intend for me to cross through that narrow gate. What I do know, is that until that time, I will live this life you have given me with a heart filled with faith, knowing that your gracious favor is all I need."

She then moved forward with her father, taking the first step toward the patio under the rose-covered pergola where Kier and her bridegroom, Park, stood waiting for her.

The End